DANCE

and

MOVEMENT SESSIONS

for Older People

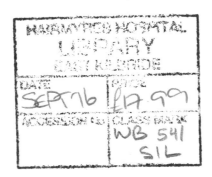

of related interest

Activities for Older People in Care Homes
A Handbook for Successful Activity Planning
Sarah Crockett
ISBN 978 1 84905 429 4
eISBN 978 0 85700 839 8

The Activity Year Book
A Week by Week Guide for Use in Elderly Day and Residential Care
Anni Bowden and Nancy Lewthwaite
ISBN 978 1 84310 963 1
eISBN 978 1 84642 889 0

How to Make Your Care Home Fun
Simple Activities for People of All Abilities
Kenneth Agar
ISBN 978 1 84310 952 5
eISBN 978 1 84642 881 4

Connecting through Music with People with Dementia
A Guide for Caregivers
Robin Rio
ISBN 978 1 84310 905 1
eISBN 978 1 84642 725 1

Playfulness and Dementia
A Practice Guide
John Killick
ISBN 978 1 84905 223 8
eISBN 978 0 85700 462 8

DANCE AND MOVEMENT SESSIONS FOR OLDER PEOPLE

A Handbook for Activity Coordinators and Carers

DELIA SILVESTER
with SUSAN FRAMPTON

Jessica Kingsley *Publishers*
London and Philadelphia

'Morning Has Broken' on p.102 written by Eleanor Farjeon, first published in *Children's Bells*, reproduced with kind permission from Oxford University Press.

'Music, Music, Music' on p.112 written by Stephan Weiss and Bernie Baum © 1949 and 1950 Cromwell Music Inc., USA assigned to TRO Essex Music Ltd. of Suite 2.07, Plaza 535, King's Road, London SW10 0SZ. International Copyright Secured. All Rights Reserved. Used by Permission.

'Pearly Shells' on p.115 written by Edwards/Pober, licensed courtesy of Eagle-I Music Ltd. on behalf of Marada Music Ltd.

First published in 2014
by Jessica Kingsley Publishers
73 Collier Street
London N1 9BE, UK
and
400 Market Street, Suite 400
Philadelphia, PA 19106, USA

www.jkp.com

Copyright © Delia Silvester and Susan Frampton 2014

Library of Congress Cataloging in Publication Data
A CIP catalog record for this book is available from the Library of Congress

British Library Cataloguing in Publication Data
A CIP catalogue record for this book is available from the British Library

ISBN 978 1 84905 470 6
eISBN 978 0 85700 846 6

Printed and bound in Great Britain by Bell and Bain Ltd, Glasgow

Contents

For the nurses of Durlston Ward, Dorset Cancer Centre, Poole Hospital NHS Foundation Trust.

Acknowledgements

First and foremost, I wish to acknowledge with profound gratitude the following residential and nursing homes and their management for the help, co-operation and opportunities they have extended in producing this book: Avonlea Nursing Home, Broadwindsor House, Coneygar Lodge, Harbour House, Careford Lodge, Whitway Nursing Home, Wolfeton Manor and Sunnybank House.

The many years I worked in these care homes gave me invaluable experience in developing methods of teaching the frail elderly, the less able and those with multiple disabilities. The input and co-operation from each of the care home managers made this book possible.

I would not have been able to complete the book without the help of Lucy Goodison and her contributions, especially to Part 1, and to her I extend my deepest appreciation.

Special thanks to Barbara Probert, Karen Jeanes, Anna Carter and Angelique Carter, the activities organisers who gave me such valuable information on the impact of regular dance, music and movement sessions.

My gratitude to Pat Yonwin and Chris Emery whose opinions, ideas, questions and critiques I always listened to and valued.

I must mention my two great friends Grace Germodo, RGN, and Madeleine Clark, RGN, who gave me both invaluable assistance on activity nursing and inspiration to devise ways of making props colourful and safe. Another friend who stood the test of time was Laura Gale, RMN, MA, with whom I had countless debates about the contribution of the arts generally and movement in particular for people with mental health issues.

Thanks to Nicky Millen, RGN, BSc (Hons), PTLLS MIO, whom I met when I first came to Dorset and by whom I had the privilege of being trained in the care of the elderly. She became such a good friend and a sounding board on all issues pertaining to training and therapeutic activities for older people.

I am privileged to have met and worked with two core members of Dance Doctors (an intergenerational and multicultural dance group with a special interest in movement for older people), Lucy Goodison and Petra Hughes. Together we complemented each other, coming as we did from three different disciplines in the fields of movement, dance, exercise and training.

I am indebted to my husband of 38 years, Nigel Silvester, who has never failed to inspire and support me over the years. He has been the driving force on every project I have undertaken. I applaud him for his patience and tenacity and for his constant reminders that problems are opportunities!

Delia Silvester,
Dorchester 2011

Editor's note

Sadly Delia died before completing this book, and without Lucy Goodison's tireless help in creating and assembling the dances and her knowledgeable and sensitive revisions to the text, honouring my promise to Delia would have been impossible. Thanks to Delia's son-in-law Rupert Streatfeild, who helped me find Delia's material, and to Emily Hurst, Alex Hurst and Petra Hughes who produced the filmed examples of two of the dances in the book. Special thanks go to Amanda Fogg for sharing her time and her professional experience of teaching dance to elderly people and to people with Parkinson's disease. Amanda kindly tested the presentation of the dances in the book and suggested invaluable amendments. Thanks too to the Stroke Association who helped fill in gaps, to Catherine Weld for her advice on presentation, and to Rachel Menzies and Allison Walker of Jessica Kingsley Publishers for their expert support.

Above all, my grateful thanks go to Malcolm Watts, whose love and generosity made it possible for me to see this project through.

From her notes, our discussions and her early drafts demonstrating Delia's urgent desire to communicate her years of experience so that more elderly people can benefit from the joy of dance, I have tried to shape this book along the lines that she would have wanted, allowing her knowledge and her passion to shine through.

Susan Frampton,
Weymouth 2012

Introduction

The purpose of this book is to encourage and enable activities coordinators, session leaders, carers and teachers to offer well-researched, safe and fun dance and movement sessions to older people living in residential and nursing homes, in sheltered accommodation and to those who are still living an independent life in their own home.

Why is this book needed?

As we live longer, our society includes a greater proportion of people confronting the symptoms of old age and trying to maintain their mobility, health and happiness. Specifically, dementia – which currently affects 800,000 people in the UK – is expected to affect one million people by 2021.

The one activity that has been proven to promote physical and mental well-being, and also to delay the onset of dementia by improving the circulation of blood to the brain, is dance.

This book gives information, guidance and step-by-step instructions for a wide range of dances to make it possible for any carer with awareness and sensitivity to run dance and movement sessions, and to improve the quality of life of thousands of older people in residential or nursing care, or in their own homes.

What are the benefits of movement and dance?

The benefits of taking part in dance and movement activities are wide-ranging and include:

Physical effects

- improves the flexibility and mobility of joints
- strengthens and tones muscles
- prevents or delays the loss of bone density
- improves balance and co-ordination
- maintains healthy cardiovascular function
- improves circulation of blood to the brain.

Benefits for everyday life

- improves posture and gait
- helps in the prevention of falls
- helps with daily physical activities and maintaining independence
- improves sleep
- delays the deterioration of brain and memory.

Psychological benefits

- improves mood and decreases anxiety
- builds confidence and self-esteem
- stimulates memories
- improves the ability to relax.

Social benefits

- prevents isolation
- offers opportunities to interact with others
- promotes appropriate physical contact with others.

Don't I need years of training to run dance sessions?

The answer is no. All you need are human qualities of thoughtfulness, imagination and commitment to caring for the needs of others.

For the purposes of this book, it is important here to make a clear distinction between exercise and dance. Exercise aims to stretch unused muscles and encourage movements that would not be undertaken voluntarily. Exercise is physical exertion for the purposes of development, training or keeping fit. For this reason, teaching or leading exercise sessions should only be undertaken by those fully trained by reputable organisations, such as EXTEND in the UK.

Dance can be defined in physical terms as the movement of any part of the body rhythmically in time to music or any other beat or accompaniment. Dance for the elderly emphatically confines itself to movements that are no more and no less than the range of movements a human being needs in order to accomplish everyday activities: the 'continuous, spontaneous movement and body language by which we all express ourselves all the time' (Crichton 1997, p.16). Dance aims to maintain that range of movement in a stimulating and joyful way. Running dance sessions requires only sensitivity and a full knowledge of contraindications and health and safety considerations.

How this book came about

The idea for this book was inspired by NAPA (National Association for the Providers of Activities for Older People) in 1998, when I first became a member. I became involved when a series of regional workshops were needed to train activities coordinators. Several research studies into caring for older people, and initiatives by regulatory bodies, had recognised the need to put activities provision at the heart of caring for older people. Consequently, the objective of running activities has developed from one of keeping residents occupied to one of maintaining quality of life, and has become embodied in the policy statements of all the best care homes.

NAPA's contribution to the training of activities coordinators since its inception cannot be overstated; it is an organisation that is unique in its concern for the quality of life of older people. I come from a cultural background in the Philippines where older people are venerated for their age and experience and I have been very impressed with what NAPA is trying to achieve. During my years as a NAPA area organiser I have been honoured to play my part.

In 1998, I was privileged to meet the founder of NAPA, Margaret Butterworth, a woman with great vision and commitment in the field of care for the elderly. Over subsequent years, a succession of women have dedicated their professional expertise to continuing Margaret's work. I would like to mention Dr Tessa Perrin, who was the NAPA training officer for a number of years and author of many books on occupational therapy and dementia; Sally Knocker, a lecturer and author who became communications director, whose newsletters and seasonal inspirations have been greatly appreciated; Sylvie Silver, who as director put NAPA on the map when she won the Daily Mail Inspirational Woman of the Year Award in 2009 for her work with NAPA and the Air Training Corps; and Sylvia Gaspar, author and resource officer for dementia and activities who has helped us in the West Dorset region.

Current government policy is to encourage older people to live in their own homes for as long as they can manage. This often means that by the time a move into a care setting becomes essential, some of their faculties will have atrophied through lack of use and growing timidity. Consequently, the job of the activities coordinator or session leader has become more challenging: the frail elderly need more attention and motivation than any other group.

Having worked as an activities coordinator, I know how useful a role music, movement, dance and exercise can play in enabling older people to continue to carry out other activities. Once movement sessions are established in a care home, the effects on mobility, flexibility, social interaction and confidence can be noticed right away. Movement is involved in every activity in life. A person who is flexible is able to hold a paintbrush or a pen but a person with very little movement is severely limited in terms of the activities they can participate in and, by extension, in their quality of life. With regular movement, dance and exercise, older people can explore a whole range of interests. Health professionals recommend that physical activities should be at least a regular weekly activity. This is not only to promote physical health but also for mental and social stimulation.

How to use this book

For this book, I have mined my own experience in order to offer as much guidance and as many ideas and suggestions as I can, to make it possible for activities coordinators to offer regular, safe and enjoyable dance, music and movement sessions to the frail and the active elderly, the less physically disabled and those living with dementia. Part 1 summarises the benefits of dance and movement for older people. Part 2 takes you step by step through the process of planning a dance or music and movement session. In Part 3, you will find detailed instructions for a selection of dances developed and tested over many years. As dances are not easily explained in words, you will also find a film demonstrating a selection of these dances on the Jessica Kingsley Publishers website (http://www.jkp.com/catalogue/book/9781849054706).

Part 1

THE BENEFITS

1

Why Movement is Important for Older People

The human body is designed to move. The joints of the human skeleton and muscle attachments enable us to complete a range of movements, such as flexion, extension, rotation and adduction. Every cell in our bodies moves constantly during our lifetime. Movement never stops even when we are at rest or asleep: the heart keeps beating, our lungs keep us breathing and our digestive, urinary and other systems of the body keep functioning. The cell, the smallest unit in the body, continues to move to produce new cells whether we are young or old. Movement only stops when we die.

Movement is automatic: when we wake in the morning we stretch to prepare ourselves for the physical exertions of the day. In fact, every normal movement in the human body is therapeutic.

You are never too old to move, dance or exercise. Ageing muscles respond well to any kind of movement. As soon as you start any type of physical activity, the effects show right away as it brings oxygen to all the cells in your body. Over a period of time the benefits increase.

In addition to offering movement sessions, the activity coordinator, session leader or carer should initiate movement with older people whenever possible: encourage people to walk if they can, instead of using a wheelchair, and guide them to breathe correctly when outside in the fresh air.

Ageing is a natural process. Maintaining a healthy and enjoyable lifestyle as we grow older is not impossible. Movement and dance can help achieve that. The ability of muscles to respond to the effects of movement is still there at any age. It is never too late to keep fit. 'Use it or lose it' is not a myth.

The different roles of movement

Movement has played many different roles in the history of human culture: it can be a means of communication, a vehicle for art or a tool for therapy.

Movement is perhaps the most ancient form of communication. Some believe that, before language, humans communicated by miming the movements they observed in nature: for example they would copy the movements of animals as a way of exchanging information during the course of hunting. Gathering together at the start of hunting expeditions and performing movements copied from animals such as galloping, jumping and stamping may be the root of social dancing and competitive sports. We may now have words but we still, consciously or unconsciously, rely heavily on interpreting body language. When elderly and disabled people have lost their power of speech they can still make themselves understood through movement, however limited: as Crichton points out, 'non-verbal movement language is a medium we use all the time' (1997, p.16).

Others believe that dance, as an expression of humans moved by transcendent power, is the earliest art form: Maria-Gabriele Wosien suggests that early humans danced to express their experience of life on every occasion, 'for joy, grief, love, fear; at sunrise, death, birth', and that the movement provided people with a deepening of their experience (1974, pp.8–9). Certainly, the expressiveness possible through dance has been utilised in all cultures and can be empowering for the dancer. Dance has been used to interpret stories, poems and songs and to create artistic performance, as well as serving to express religious and spiritual beliefs and practices. The potential healing effect of these practices is increasingly acknowledged in our culture, and in the UK the discipline of dance movement psychotherapy is now recognised by the National Health Service (NHS).

2

Moving in Old Age

How It Helps

Physical effects

On 2 February 2010, the BBC convened a panel of independent experts, chaired by the Alzheimer's Society, which evaluated more than 70 research papers and articles about the causes and prevention of dementia. The panel concluded that, although you cannot alter your age or your genes, there are lifestyle changes that can combat the development of dementia.

Clive Ballard, Director of Research for the Alzheimer's Society and Professor of Age Related Disorders at the Institute of Psychiatry, King's College London, stated officially for the first time what carers, occupational therapists and dance therapists have long believed: that exercise can counteract dementia.

Many people believe that doing puzzles like Sudoku keeps the brain alive, but Professor Ballard made it clear that the jury is still out on whether such brain games, including crosswords, can help. He stated: 'Actually, if people are trying to protect themselves a bit against Alzheimer's disease, looking after the body is probably more helpful than looking after the brain' (BBC News, 2 February 2010).

To help protect against dementia at least 30 minutes of exercise, five times a week, is recommended. This does not have to involve a trip to the gym: any form of exercise that gets the heart pumping will do the trick. Exercise is believed to help by promoting blood flow to the brain. There is also growing evidence that regular exercise has other health effects such as promoting cell and tissue repair mechanisms, including the growth of new cells in the brain.

Stimulating blood flow to other parts of the body reduces stiffness and pain, while the exercising of muscles mobilises joints and promotes strength and flexibility – thus improving a person's skill and safety in performing daily activities. Jerome describes how 'the most minimal of movements, such as gentle swaying from foot to foot, is a means of finding physical balance' (1999, p.23). Even facial muscles need to move, as is often seen in Eastern forms of exercise. Facial exercises help clear air passages in the nose and throat to improve breathing and facilitate oxygen distribution to the rest of the body.

Witnessing movement also has a health-giving effect. Session leaders notice that observers often start to move slightly or join in after a while (Kindell and Amans 2003), but, even without moving, recent studies have shown that watching a dance sequence activates the same areas of the brain that would be used in performing that sequence. Visual stimuli can activate neural pathways to muscles in the limbs (Pruszynski *et al.* 2010), causing an involuntary response. So, even if an individual's own movement is restricted or non-existent, there can be stimulation simply from watching someone else dance.

Psychological and social effects

In non-Western cultures, dance also serves other functions often lost sight of in our contemporary culture. For elderly people, movement and dance can be a source of stimulation that lifts the spirits, transforms feelings, and enhances memory, cognitive function, communication, awareness and self-esteem. Aches and pains recede, human losses can be reconfigured and experience can be reshaped by the powerful effect of the human body in movement.

There are a number of ways in which this can happen. One way is through dance's mood-changing capacity. Dance is capable of affecting atmosphere, cheering people and shifting their feelings. A study of residents in seventeen residential homes showed that 40 per cent were depressed, although this depression was recognised by staff in less than a quarter of cases (Schneider and Mann 1997). Watching or taking part in movement and dance, however minimally, can make people feel different, lift depression and effect a temporary but significant improvement in well-being (Perrin 1998).

This works by making people more aware of their own bodies and physical reality. Bringing awareness lower down into the body – away from the mind which may not be working so well – can give elderly people a more solid place in the world. The sense of self is strengthened by a focus on contact with the ground and a connection with the world through gravity (Jerome 1999). Such an experience is even more important for people who are detached from reality because of dementia, suspended in an unfamiliar world which can be incomprehensible and frightening.

Touch is important to everyone, and especially elderly people who may have lost their partners and be living far away from their wider family. People need to be touched, stroked, cuddled and massaged; this is not always possible, but dance and movement can counteract isolation by offering opportunities for bodies to interact safely. Movement activities provide a comfortable context for elderly people to make appropriate physical contact with their own body and with others. Body boundaries are affirmed through physical touch and the sense of self can be strengthened by contact with other people (Jerome 1999). Circle dance, for example, 'provides the opportunity to touch, hold, move together gently and be part of a group' (Heymanson 2009, p.13).

Moreover, communicating through movement is not dependent on speech. Communication that is simple and physical provides an alternative means of dialogue where problems with word retrieval mean that language is failing and where there are other difficulties with interpersonal exchanges. The interaction generated by dancing as a shared non-verbal activity can enhance relationships and promote bonding as a group. This has also been observed between couples (Heymanson 2009); and relationships with staff can improve after dancing together (Kindell and Amans 2003). At the same time, the non-verbal activity can stimulate language use, giving people something to chat about (Jerome 1999): 'The moving loosens up the words' (Crichton 1997).

Movement and dance can also contribute to the affirmation of cultural identity. Shared dances and specific repeated movements can serve to remind people of their race, class or place of origin: who they are, what they believe in and what their values are. Dance can be a significant cultural marker. It can make a statement about roots for people who have been historically displaced: an example is the survival in the UK of traditions of Indian folk dance. It can celebrate your own or another's national identity, as – famously – with Irish dancing, but also with traditional circle dances from Eastern Europe, Greece, Israel and South America. It can awaken images of a shared, idealised past, as with maypole dancing. It can make a link to periods of history which older people have themselves lived through, as with the foxtrot or jitterbug: familiar music can elicit a spontaneous movement response since often the body memory of a certain style of dancing survives intact when other things are forgotten (Coaten 2001; Lamont 2008).

Music is in itself proven to have a very beneficial effect (Hulme *et al.* 2010). The parts of the brain receptive to music can be more resistant to decay, so listening to music offers a valuable opportunity to experience pleasure. Rhythm is repetitive and containing: in the world of a dementia sufferer, where things may seem confusing and unsafe, musical rhythm can give a sense of cohesion and reassurance. Jerome suggests that in circle dancing 'the rocking and gentle repetitive movements…communicate acceptance directly and without words in the manner of early attachment experiences' (1999, p.21).

Stimulation from sound and activity gives the opportunity for participation and also for some simple memory-training in learning steps if appropriate. In this way, dance can support increased concentration in the here and now (Donald and Hall 1999). There can be much satisfaction in mastering a short routine. If that is not possible, there is the opportunity simply to follow on. Elderly people can become bored and frustrated because of their inability to do things, and movement provides an opportunity to take part at whatever level is appropriate for them.

Reminiscence work using familiar music and songs can trigger long-term life memories, which are known to be more resilient than short-term memories. This gives pleasure and a connection to the past, particularly important if through dementia there is a loss of a sense of personhood (Coaten 2001).

As part of such projects, costumes and props can make an important contribution for people with dementia who think in pictures. Using props can also enhance movement sessions in other ways. A giant band of stretch cloth can begin to connect group members in co-operative movements when direct touch would be too confrontational (Donald and Hall 1999); batting a balloon around a circle, waving twizzle sticks or wafting scarves can be relaxing (Crichton 1997; Perrin 1998).

In care provision for the elderly, there is much awareness of the importance of memory. But quality of life in a residential or day care setting does not lie only in honouring memories from years gone by. It also lies in generating, where possible, new landmarks and new memories. This is why the dances described in this book include not only the familiar and those that relate to the past, but also new ones, so that there is an ongoing expansion and enrichment of experience. Follow-up from a dance session need not be restricted to discussion of past personal histories, but can contribute significantly to what is happening in the present.

Difficult emotional states can sometimes be helped by movement. Some elderly people living with dementia have a tendency to wander; in such cases joining in dance or movement work can give a positive outlet for their agitation (Kindell and Amans 2003). The act of moving or dancing can shift someone into a different frame of mind, and pent-up frustration can be released in a safe way, for example by rolling a ball across the circle or pulling on a scarf (Crichton 1997). It is not only that exercise releases into the body endorphins which can promote feelings of euphoria; it is also that initiating and experiencing movement can give a sense of empowerment. People with dementia describe a loss of self-esteem as they lose abilities and independence (Gillies 1997); while exercise sessions can be directive and hard to follow, dance can allow people to express themselves and move in a 'failure free' way (Kindell and Amans 2003, p.20).

'Freestyle' dancing (which, like all dancing, can be done from a wheelchair) is an especially good format for allowing the autonomy of self-expression to people who spend so much time fitted into the timetables of others. In the early twentieth century, Isadora Duncan was the inspiration for modern dance when she turned away from steps and gestures imposed from outside, as in traditional ballet. Instead, she looked to the roots of dance as a sacred art and within that developed free and authentic movements inspired by folk dances and nature (Duncan 1988 [1928]). The focus was not on external forms, but on 'movement's internal initiation' in people and their feelings, giving participants the opportunity to pay attention to their impulses, create their own movements in the moment and 'experience the self' (Steinman 1986, pp.78–79, p.82). This can be pleasurable, enriching and deeply validating of self-worth.

On occasion, movement can also play a valuable role in honouring and exploring emotions: it can provide a symbolic representation of more complex or challenging aspects of human relationship. Crichton notes that the 'overwhelming feelings of loss, confusion, frustration and powerlessness caused by dementia often flow too deep for words. Dance can speak volumes' (1997, p.16). She argues for an approach that 'gives clear structures to contain the expression of these strong, often uncomfortable emotions' (1997, p.16). Sometimes, as in morris dancing, movement enacts themes of conflict in a safe way. Donald and Hall describe how in one session underlying aggression 'found outlet in the energetic bouncing of a physio ball to each other – an example of how movement can channel and express problematic emotion' (1999, p.27). Freestyle dancing, in a safe context and with safe equipment such as light scarves, can give a valuable opportunity for participants to bring out preoccupations from their inner world. Themes such as support, collaboration, separation or loss can be expressed in movement terms; this makes them accessible to being acknowledged and, if appropriate, discussed as part of ongoing group activities.

Sensory pleasure can be derived not only from music but also from the experience of moving and from the act of participating, which enriches life in the moment. When elderly people find that their functions of memory, planning and interpretation are becoming impaired, taking pleasure in the present can be a mainstay of life. Session leaders find that dance can help people 'express their joie de vivre and celebrate the richness of their life experiences through individual and interactive movements' (Donald and Hall 1999, p.27).

Spiritual satisfaction

Writing about dementia care, Jaaniste has noted that recently 'there has been a growth of consciousness that creative activity can contribute to people's health and well-being and that the area of spirituality is integral, and perhaps even central, to psycho-social health and a sense of well-being' (2011, p.16). Spirituality in this context is not necessarily aligned with religion but is more holistic, referring to personal, affective and thoughtful qualities and recognising connectedness to others and love of the earth (Jaaniste 2011). Although dance does not play a significant role within the West's dominant religious traditions, there is an uplifting, spiritual potential in witnessing and participating in dance, expressed in qualities of celebration, ceremony and connection. Circle dance in particular is seen as a way of connecting to the spirit of self and of others, but many dances offer an experience of participation that can expand the spirit. This can make a valuable contribution to enriching the lives of elderly people, whose horizons may in other ways be limited due to illness or lack of mobility.

Short-circuiting the written and spoken word, movement work also allows the possibility of sharing physically in aspects of the world which are not within our literal experience. Whether this is the buoyancy of a bird in flight, the delicacy of leaves in the wind or the strength of a tree trunk, it allows a route to connect with the natural environment around us.

A sense of spirituality can be important in sustaining people who are no longer functioning fully in the complex outer layer of personality that used to characterise them. Jerome suggests that 'the transformative qualities of the dance lie in its capacity to hold and hold on to the person who is in the process of slipping away' (1999, p.23). Travelling deeper than the conflicting emotions that have woven through their history and life experiences, some people living with dementia are on a journey into the core of their being; music and movement can help them on that journey.

Conclusion

In short, dance not only has a positive effect on physical health and body functioning, but can also, in a very immediate way, help individuals to find and retain their place in the world: their place in their own body, their place in history, their place in relationships, their place in society and their place in nature and the cosmos. These reference points are needed not only by elderly people who may be displaced from their cognitive functions or displaced in residential homes, but by us all.

Part 2

THE DANCE SESSION

The key to a successful dance session is preparation. A good session leader will be highly organised: you will have conducted risk assessments and updated your knowledge of the participants, considered health and safety issues, prepared the venue and planned the session in advance.

3

Preparing Yourself

It is important that you feel confident in your ability to deliver the session. If you are a trained dancer or a creative person it will not be difficult for you to develop your own ideas for music and movement and dance sessions. If you are not, don't despair as there are many opportunities for you to gain experience of dance sessions put together by others. I highly recommend that you explore some of the following opportunities before embarking on your own sessions:

- In village halls and community centres you will find regular classes on yoga, dance yoga, ballroom dancing, belly dancing, Pilates, Zumba and so on.

- In local colleges you will find classes taught in tap, jazz and modern dance.

- Organisations for specific types of dance, like circle dancing, Dances of Universal Peace, Scottish dancing, line dancing and morris dancing run regular classes and workshops.

- If you intend to use sign language, you can enrol for classes in adult education centres in your area. You could also contact Deaf Clubs or the Royal National Institute for the Blind (RNIB) and ask for their help. Members will be able to help you interpret the songs you want to use in your sessions. You can attend workshops or you can buy the basic signing DVDs available.

- Arts centres are a good source of dance classes for ethnic dances such as African, Asian and Middle Eastern dance.

- Becoming a member of a community dance organisation like the Foundation for Community Dance in the UK will give you access to a range of workshops and training in your area. It is also a great way of networking locally.

- You could become a member of a small dance group yourself; you can find out what is available near you by checking out national arts councils like Arts Council England (see other national/federal councils listed under 'Organisations' in Appendix 2). Arts Council England supports dance and health initiatives as well as professional dance.

- YouTube offers many clips of instructors demonstrating various dances so that you can learn online and pick out moves you enjoy to pass on to others in the sessions you run.

- If you are someone who is inspired by books, the Bibliography includes several general books on dance that include pictures and ideas you could draw on.

In Part 3 you will find step-by-step instructions for dances that I have developed over the years with my colleagues in Dance Doctors; watching a selection of these demonstrated online (http://www.jkp.com/catalogue/book/9781849054706) will help even more.

4

Preparing Your Venue

The room you use for the dance and movement session should have:

- good ventilation

- good lighting

- chairs that are sturdy and support the back, ideally without arms so that participants can move freely. However, for participants with impaired balance and co-ordination use chairs with arms

- cushions for clients whose feet do not reach the floor, as feet should not be left hanging

- toilets located nearby.

Prepare your room like this:

- Arrange the room so that there is a seat for every participant, even if some participants intend to stand during parts of the session.

- Don't place chairs facing strong light from a window as participants will not be able to see you.

- Arrange the chairs in a semicircle.

- As session leader, you should place yourself in the middle of the semicircle so that you can be seen clearly and so that you can see every participant and check that no one is distressed when executing a move.

- Give priority to participants suffering from sensory loss when you allocate seats.

- Place participants with tunnel vision at the mid-point of the semicircle of chairs.

- Place clients with hearing aids away from the sound system. Hearing aids are sensitive and the person wearing one does not need the sound amplified. On the other hand, clients without a hearing aid but who are still hard of hearing prefer the sound to be loud. You must find a happy compromise; it can be tricky!

- Ensure that there is an arm's length distance either side of someone who is known to become agitated sometimes. In this situation it is best to ensure you have members of staff helping in the session.

5

Thinking About Equipment

Treat all equipment and props for movement and dance sessions as potentially dangerous. Health and safety must be your priority whenever you use equipment or make props for use in the dances.

- Put all equipment away after every session. There are two reasons for this. First, to avoid accidents: people with impaired vision or with poor balance and co-ordination can easily trip and fall over equipment left lying around. Second, participants living with dementia will believe seeing something new every time they have a session.

- When you connect your sound system, ensure electrical leads are secured out of sight and are not left lying where someone might trip over them.

- Keep in mind participants with sensory impairment when you make props as well as those who are physically disabled.

- Be careful when you hand out controversial props like rhythm sticks. Make sure you know the mood of your participants on the day.

- Ensure you can account for all your props when you gather them up after you have finished using them. If people with dementia refuse to hand back a piece of equipment, enlist the help of staff to get it back; leaving a prop with a participant could be dangerous.

- Walking frames can be useful in dance sessions. Not only do they help participants with issues like balance but also they can give confidence, and if you can encourage someone to stand for at least some of the dances, the benefit will be greater on their overall health and well-being. Do make sure that the frame height of the walking frame is correct for each individual; the wrong height can cause backache and give them reason not to participate in the future. Coaching participants on a one-to-one basis in how to use the walking frame during a session is highly recommended.

6

Preparing For Your Participants

Risk assessments

Conduct a risk assessment for each participant, including respite care participants, before *every* session and keep your own records. Information you need to have includes: whether someone has had a heart attack, stroke or any recent injury; their ability or not to stand or move their arms, hands, fingers, legs, feet and face; how well they can see, hear and speak; whether they have enjoyed singing and dancing; and whether they have dementia.

- Official risk assessments are required by regulatory bodies; make sure you see them.

- Do you need to adapt the movements you used last time? Over a period of time a person's health situation can change as a consequence of degenerative diseases; you need to know whether any of your participants have suffered a stroke, heart attack, fall, macular degeneration or any further advance in diseases like Parkinson's since you last saw them.

- Check whether any of the participants are receiving treatment from a physiotherapist and if so, consult the physiotherapist.

- Ensure you have enough staff to help you during the session.

- Check that any props you intend to use meet health and safety guidelines. If you intend to use fresh flowers or fresh branches with leaves attached in a session, check for allergies among participants.

Contraindicated and controversial moves

A contraindicated move is a movement that is best avoided by an individual or group; a controversial move is a movement that is potentially contraindicated, that is, potentially risky but could be acceptable. Revise these contraindications before each session and keep your knowledge up to date.

Always try to find an alternative to any movement that might be contraindicated or controversial. Remember that a movement might be contraindicated for some but not for others.

It is good practice to remind your class about contraindications from time to time, especially between dances.

All movements should be slow at first. Sudden movements are confusing. All movements should be broken down into simple and achievable parts and should suit participants' abilities and ranges of movement.

- Never jerk the neck. A neck warm-up must always be gentle. Do not start your session warm-up with head or neck exercises. Instead, exercise shoulders first to warm up the muscles at the base of the neck. For participants with dementia, who will have a short memory span, it is advisable to place a towel around the neck to prevent them from over-extending. Over-extending can cause dizziness and even a blackout. Head circling must be avoided. Lateral flexion of the neck (moving or tipping the head sideways) must be done very slowly. Remember our necks become very delicate as we age. Do not keep the head down for too long as this can cause dizziness.

- Never raise the arms above the head before you have completed a thorough warm-up as raising the arms like this makes the heart work harder. Participants suffering from angina or asthma, participants with breathing problems or those who may have suffered a heart attack in the past should avoid raising their arms above their heads at all times. Ensure you always have participants' inhalers and medication to hand before you start. It would be a good idea to give the responsibility for medications to a particular person during the session.

- Breathe, breathe and breathe. Often, intense concentration can cause participants to forget to breathe correctly. Do not do any breathing exercises for too long as it can cause hyperventilation and can lead to dizziness. It strains the heart and is not helpful for asthma or angina sufferers. Also breathing exercises must not be too deep, especially for the frail elderly, so always ensure that the in-breath is matched by an out-breath of the same duration. Breathing exercises should be performed in a sitting position.

- Participants with hip, shoulder and knee replacements must be monitored at all times. There should be no jerky movements. Participants with hip or knee replacements should not lift the knee higher than hip level. Do watch for participants moving either leg too far to the side. Participants with hip replacements should never cross their legs or ankles. They should avoid twisting the hip and never turn or swivel on the ball of their foot but take small steps to turn around. Participants with shoulder replacements cannot raise their arms and hands above their heads. Show them how to place their arms in an oblique position (halfway between front and side) or suggest they raise their arms as far as shoulder level.

- Never raise both legs together with knees straight. This is too stressful for the back and particularly bad for people with back problems or for people suffering from arthritis in the lower limbs or the upper or lower spine.

- Do not include too many repetitions in your dance routines. It strains the joints, makes muscles too tired and can cause inflammation. A maximum of 16 counts is acceptable.

- Do include some flexibility exercises for hands, including thumbs, wrists and elbows to promote mobility. Not only will this develop strength but it will also improve grip, which will help with other activities. With flexible hands, clients can participate in art and craft work and be encouraged to undertake familiar household activities like folding clothes, tidying up and watering house plants. Most of all, though, they will be able to dance and move with confidence. Sufferers from osteoporosis of the hands or wrists should not shake their hands vigorously; they should be encouraged to wave instead.

- If possible, warm-up exercises are more effective barefoot because you can emphasise the range of movement without the restriction of socks and slippers. I recommend that participants do wear shoes for dancing to protect the feet, and especially if the dance requires tapping or stamping the foot. Avoid slippery shoes and slippers with no grip which could cause the participant to slip.

- Clothes must be comfortable to move in. Avoid tight clothes and trousers that are wide and loose around the hem.

- Allow from one to two hours after a meal before embarking on a dance or movement session. Moving too soon after a meal can cause vomiting or stomach pain.

Reminders for specific disabilities

Diabetes: Ensure that the participant has eaten and that any medication is near to hand. Make sure you do not tire them out.

Hearing: The first sign of age-related hearing loss is when someone has difficulty understanding what people are saying to them. At this stage they will also find it difficult to recognise high-frequency sounds. Hearing impairment can affect socialisation and relationships within the group as it can often be mistaken for rudeness. Be aware that music might obstruct your instructions for people with impaired hearing.

Heart conditions, angina and other related breathing problems: If a participant complains of chest pains, stop immediately and consult a doctor.

Hiatus hernia: The most common types of hernia are the inguinal (groin) hernia and the femoral hernia. The inguinal hernia is more common in men than in women. Although stretching should be encouraged, do avoid bending the trunk forward and be careful with raising the knees as this can cause the hernia to bulge.

Neurological diseases: Sufferers from Parkinson's disease, multiple sclerosis, motor neurone disease and strokes should always aim for smooth movements and avoid fatigue or over-stimulation. The session leader can help improve mobility by moving the participant's affected limbs for them.

Osteoarthritis: It is advisable to work through the full range of movement for every joint in the body. However, if a joint is hot and inflamed, do not exercise. If a joint is swollen but not hot (that is, not inflamed), encourage the sufferer to participate in the session but to stay within the limits of their pain.

Osteoporosis: Sufferers from osteoporosis in their hands or wrists should wave as an alternative to shaking their hands vigorously. Weight-bearing exercise is recommended for those suffering from osteoporosis, so do encourage them to stand to participate in dance and movement sessions whenever possible. It also helps to work through the full range of movement for each joint. Strong bones can only be maintained by regular exercise.

Rheumatoid arthritis: Ensure that clients work within their pain limits. If there is an inflammation in the joint (commonly referred to as a 'flare-up'), it becomes stiff and swollen. Cut the more strenuous movements but don't stop exercising; instead work through a range of gentle movement for the affected joint.

Sight: Of all the senses, sight deterioration is the one impairment that affects our everyday lives most. It deprives us of activities we might once have enjoyed like reading and the pursuit of our favourite hobbies – or even just watching television. It can also be a major cause of falls and other injuries. Participants with deteriorating vision can recognise only red, yellow and white, so it is good practice for session leaders to wear these colours. Wearing white gloves as well will be helpful to those suffering from macular degeneration because they see white more easily than any other colour.

Stroke: Work on the stiffness of the affected part of the body. Encourage the participant to use the good hand or foot to assist the affected part. Encourage bilateral movement using both sides of the body. Fatigue is an issue with stroke patients, so beware of over-stimulation.

Touch: The sense of touch seems to be the least problematic in our everyday activities, although ageing can lessen the sense of feeling in our hands as well as in other parts of the body due to the slower responses of nerve endings. Appropriate touch during movement sessions can be very beneficial.

7

Planning and Running a Session

Use a range of movements

A well-planned dance session can provide the full range of types of movement that the body needs to stay healthy.

Strengthening movements build the body's strength, usually through some form of resistance training. For the active and physically fit, strengthening exercises include walking, swimming, jogging, climbing stairs, dancing and some competitive sports. For the frail elderly, the best way to incorporate strengthening exercises into your session is to include dances that involve walking and dances that utilise props.

Stretching movements improve the flexibility and mobility of joints. Stretching should be performed when the body is fully warmed-up and performing the dances themselves will provide a range of stretching movements. Specific stretching movements are recommended for the cooling-down period once the dances themselves are finished.

Balance movements are helpful in preventing falls and injuries resulting from falls; these moves are normally directed towards the lower part of the body. Examples of balancing movements include marching (standing or seated); moving your body weight from left to right and vice versa (seated participants can achieve the same effect by lifting first the left buttock and then the right); walking naturally but with awareness of your shoulders being balanced on either side; and, for standing clients, standing first on one foot, then the other.

Endurance movements work the cardiovascular system, building and maintaining staying power. Working hard throughout a dance session is an enjoyable way to develop endurance. Typically marching, sidestepping, and alternate knee lifting provide a good workout for the cardiovascular system.

The structure of your session

Your session should consist of three parts:

1. warm-up

2. dance section

3. cool down.

Warm-up

Best *et al.* (2010), in their guidelines for exercise after a stroke, suggest that for a session lasting an hour the warm-up section should last between 15 and 20 minutes. The idea is to enhance circulation and mobility before embarking on the dance section, and also to introduce some of the basic movement patterns you will use in the dance section. Instructions for a warm-up are included in Part 3.

Dance section

In Chapter 9, you will find a list of different dances by type to help you choose suitable material for the middle part of your session. Ensure that you start with something lyrical and simple to help build confidence. It is best to introduce only one new dance per session.

Cool down

All sessions should end with a cool down that includes some rhythmical activities to lower the heart rate gradually and prepare the body for some flexibility stretches to improve posture and range of movement, and to prevent long-term injury. Flexibility stretches should include stretches to the calf muscles, chest muscles, back of thigh muscles, side of trunk muscles and neck, arm and shoulder muscles.

Running a session

1. Be pleasant at all times.

2. Speak clearly.

3. Keep in mind what you know about the participants' individual physical limitations.

4. Ensure you know any likes and dislikes; for example, a member of the group may dislike certain songs because of unpleasant associations.

5. Always praise participants when they are doing well. Remember to praise them between each phase of the dance as they master the movements step by step.

6. Demonstrate the moves clearly and patiently because their response depends on the way you execute the movements. It is always good to demonstrate the moves in a mirroring position, meaning if you start a move with your left hand, participants will start with their right.

7. Dress appropriately. Don't wear jewellery. Older people have delicate skin, prone to tearing and bruising easily, and if you are wearing a ring when you hold hands you may hurt them.

8

Choosing and Using Music

The magic of music

Exercise in silence can feel like a chore. But add music and something magical happens. As well as being a great mood enhancer, the healing effects of music can be skillfully utilised in dance and music and movement sessions. According to the Alzheimer's Society, 'Hidden in the fun are activities which build on the well-known preserved memory for song and music in the brain. Even when many memories are hard to retrieve, music is especially easy to recall' (www.alzheimers.org.uk/singingforthebrain 2013). Music triggers memories and can contribute to reminiscence work. But above all, music provokes the body to move.

Recordings of natural phenomena like waves, rain, wind or the rippling of a stream are great for promoting relaxation. Even recordings of cats, dogs and birds are useful; notice how participants will move their bodies and their heads to look towards the direction of the sound. Just moving the body to the right and left for the satisfaction of identifying where the sounds come from may herald the start of a willingness to move the whole body. Dance practitioners have often remarked on how people with dementia reconnect body and mind in the short space of time that it takes for a familiar piece of music to play – at least for the duration of the piece if not for longer. Sometimes you will observe only the tiniest change in facial expression in a person with advanced dementia and who has lost the ability to move their body completely, but you will know that music is working its magic.

The ground rules for using recorded music: legal issues

We have access to a vast resource of recorded music to use in our sessions, from CDs and from the Internet. It is important therefore that you buy the appropriate annual licences before you use any recorded music in your sessions. You will need both:

- a Public Performance Licence (PPL)

- a Performing Rights for Music Licence (PRS).

The tariff for both is dependent on the average number of participants per session and the number of sessions you run per annum.

In addition, if you make up your own CD with selected recorded tracks or download selected tracks to an MP3 device or similar, you will need additional licences from both PPL and PRS. The contact details for both organisations are online and are included in the reference section of this book and I strongly advise you to contact them directly to ascertain which licences you will need and which tariff you must pay.

Selecting music for sessions

For many of the dances in Part 3, you will need a music recording to accompany the dance. Although I make some recommendations, you can choose your own; however, you do need to make sure that the tempo is slower than average. For general music and movement sessions you will need to select music yourself. Here are some guidelines to help you choose:

- Older people with sensory loss or dementia and others with short attention spans respond well to music with very strong accents.

- For music and movement sessions with able-bodied participants, there are CDs pre-recorded by dance organisations that provide music for warm-up, a main movement section and then music for cooling down. If you have a licence for making up your own playlist on CD or MP3 player, you can download tracks to your computer and then slow the tempo for less able-bodied participants.

- Music with lyrics encourages older people to sing along and you need to be aware that singing along can distract them from following the movements you are demonstrating – many will not be able to sing and move at the same time. As session leaders it is important that we allow participants to sing if they choose. Not only will singing exercise the thoracic region but it may also trigger memories to help with reminiscence work, lead to social interaction with others in the group and promote a sense of belonging. The Alzheimer's Society in the UK, recognising the value of singing for older people, provides a service, Singing for the Brain, which uses singing to bring people together in a friendly and stimulating social environment and you may want to check out what is available in your area.

9

Choosing Dances

You can select which dances to include in your session using a wide range of criteria. You can choose by type or by theme, or you can choose to link your dance with other arts and crafts projects or reminiscence work.

All the types of dances listed below can be adapted for chair-based or bed-based exercise and have been tried and tested during 11 years of practice.

Dances by type

Creative dance/improvisation

For expressive, improvised dance there is no formal choreography. Participants just move their bodies as they please, according to the rhythm of the music or the beat of percussive instruments. This type of dance encourages creativity and the expression of emotions and is always very popular with people living with dementia. Freestyle dance, sometimes called free dance or creative improvisation, frees the dancer/mover from the limitations and tensions of performing formal steps, encouraging relaxation and pure creativity. Colours, fabrics and props can foster spatial awareness and expression. Creative dances can channel or interpret the life stories of the participants; greater emotional and physical connection among the participants is often evident after the session. Pick music that suits the mood on the day. Improvised movement can be subtly directed with suggestions for types of movements and moods or themes: in Part 3 there are some ideas for themes to get people started.

Circle dancing/Greek dancing

Dancing in circles is the oldest known dance form. Circle dance, or sacred circle dance, is a mixture of traditional dances from all over Europe and the Balkans. These dances are usually performed in a circle but can easily be performed standing or sitting in a line, hand-holding distance apart. Holding hands boosts confidence, balance and co-ordination but also bridges distance, enabling connection between people often isolated by their age or disability. The movements themselves are simple and repetitive and make Greek and circle dancing ideal for participants with memory problems. Easily adapted for seated clients, Greek and circle dances can be reflective or lively and energetic and can be performed to various kinds of modern and traditional music – to songs, chants and even to mantras. I include an example in Part 3.

Dances of universal peace

These dances are meditative and spiritual. What makes them interesting for this purpose is the diversity of the dance moves, as many countries have their own version of chants, songs and meditative exercises. They may also include sacred phrases, psalms or the scriptures of the spiritual practice of the country of origin. This suits eclectic New Age beliefs in the values of multiculturalism. For some participants such dances could be controversial, especially if someone is a devout Christian. You might therefore find some of your participants unable to join in with these particular dances because of their religious convictions; it is important that you give them the choice. At first, the dances of universal peace were very popular in dance camps; subsequently, because of their holistic approach, interest in them spread to different care settings such as nursing and residential homes, hospices and day centres as well as prisons. The emphasis is not on how the movements look, but on participation and spiritual experience. Steps are easy to learn and the movements convey a celebration of life; in origin they are used as a focus in weddings and other gatherings that reflect social events in the community. Part 3 includes an example, 'Step Softly on the Earth', which is an adaptation of a Native American sacred dance.

Hawaiian dances

Hawaiian dances have always been especially popular in all the homes where I have taught. I include 'Pearly Shells' as an example of a Hawaiian dance in Part 3, because its combination of rhythm, melody and expressiveness, as with all hula dances, is infectious and joyful – as well as simple to learn. I often notice audience and observers joining in! Hula dances were handed down to the Hawaiians by the Polynesians who were the first inhabitants of the islands. The dances originated in religious ceremonies but are now performed for entertainment. Every hula movement has a meaning; this is expressed through the hands imitating the movement of the trees, plants and animals as well as other natural phenomena like waves and storms. In fact, hula moves are like a sign language and I have often substituted a move from British Sign Language (BSL) or Makaton where a traditional hula move might prove a little too complicated. Another positive feature of Hawaiian dancing is that simple props can add to the enjoyment: simplified versions of grass skirts, neck garlands (leis) and flowers for the hair are easy to make, and add another activity to your repertoire for arts and crafts sessions.

Traditional folk dances of the British Isles

Elderly people, especially in rural communities, enjoy traditional folk dancing – often because they learned the steps as children (see Rippon 1975 for examples). It makes the dances and their props invaluable for reminiscence work. Handkerchiefs, ribbons, adapted sticks and bells are all easy to find or make, and add to the sense of occasion. You could, again, make garlands of flowers in arts and crafts sessions. To help residents maintain mobility in their fingers, hands and arms a simple table-based exercise would be to fill spring baskets with petals and encourage participants to scatter and gather the petals.

In Part 3, there are two simplified morris dances; performing them on May Day, or indeed any time during May, highlights the arrival of spring and all the positive associations to do with the start of a new cycle. Morris dancing has been popular in Britain since the fifteenth century. There are many regional variations, evident in the colours used in costumes or in the percussion instruments played. It's useful to be aware of the variation for your own region.

Spiritual dances

Eight years ago, I noticed the emergence of liturgical dancing in Christian churches. My first experience was when I attended a service at the Holy Trinity Brompton church in Knightsbridge, London. I was pleasantly surprised when young and old stood up and started to move as they sang the hymns; this gave another level of meaning to the service. The second experience was something very different. It was held in a small Christian church in the little town of Bridport in Dorset, and the congregation waved pieces of floaty fabric and flags depicting religious images. The effect was the same.

Liturgical dances can express different emotions such as love, sadness, fear and anger, as well as thanksgiving and praise. The dance can be accompanied by a reading from the scriptures, religious songs, psalms and poems as well as music. What these dances offer participants is the opportunity to reconnect with the spiritual element of their lives. You do have to be particularly sensitive, however, to the religious beliefs of your participants and adapt your music and texts accordingly (see Hunter 2002 for ideas). You may want to adapt your preparation of the room to make it suitable for a more meditative and reflective session. In Part 3 I include a dance to accompany the popular Christian hymn 'Morning Has Broken'.

Line dancing

Line dancing is performed to country and western music. Participants all face forward and there is no physical contact between participants. Although primarily a step dance, it can be adapted to involve the upper body (see our example in Part 3). Using cowboy hats and scarves as props can help to ensure movement of the torso and can add to creating an atmosphere.

Novelty dances

Participants will already know some of these dances and that is a bonus for when you want to focus on moving well rather than on learning new movements. The dances are light-hearted and funny, and with their familiar movements work well with older people and those with dementia; the rhythm is easy to identify and the movements are simple. Here are some examples with the era in which they were first popular:

- 1940s: the Hokey Cokey
- 1960s: the Twist, the Chicken Dance, the Mashed Potato and the Madison
- 1970s: 'Birdie Song', 'YMCA', 'Agadoo', 'Time Warp' and 'Superman'
- 1980s: 'Walk Like an Egyptian'
- 1990s: the Macarena
- 2000s: the Ketchup Dance.

I include 'Time Warp' (from *The Rocky Horror Show*, 1973) above because, although it will be unfamiliar to older people now in their 80s or 90s, it has a strong beat and the movement instructions are contained in the lyrics. Finger bopping, the Swim (Hawaiian or Polynesian music works well for this one) and the Hitch Hike are novelty dances that can be easily adapted for seated participants.

The Hand Jive is another novelty dance that participants may have performed at some point in their lives. It does as it says and concentrates movement in the upper body. I often call hand jive a memory dance because it does challenge participants to remember the movements (see instructions in Part 3).

Miming to a song is always popular and simple. Movements can describe boxes, cars, mountains or people playing musical instruments. You can make it a game, like Charades, or a dance with background music. Everyday activities – ironing, cooking, cleaning carpets, gardening, folding clothes, sewing and bathing – make good subjects for dances; in Part 3 you will find 'Dashing Away with the Smoothing Iron' as a popular example.

The Locomotion and the Conga are follow-the-leader dances and are great for fostering social interaction. I have noticed that some clients do not communicate with the person nearest to them even if they have been living together in the same care home for a number of years – they will even avoid eye contact. But the most surprising effect of music and dance is that as soon as they hold hands to dance they start talking to each other – if only to point out errors in each other's footwork! Some do remain friends after the session but many retreat back into their shells until the next dance session.

With careful planning, most of the fad dances can be structured to suit the older person with disabilities. The best advice is to listen to all the music carefully and note the tempo or the beat as well as the lyrics; it is easier to teach the moves when you are familiar with the lyrics. Some of the dance crazes, such as disco, have footwork that involves synchronising with hand movements. These look complicated and can be off-putting for seated clients and for those with short memory spans so you must concentrate on learning one movement before moving on to the next.

Tap dancing

Tap dancing has also been a favourite in my dance sessions. Many residents will have enjoyed watching tap dancing at some point in their lives. It always provokes a mood of nostalgia, whether it is classical tap of the sort performed by Fred Astaire and Ginger Rogers or has a modern jazz twist as performed by

Gene Kelly. Tap dancing originated in the UK as a combination of clog dancing and Irish jigs. American tap, on the other hand, originated from the black slave community, and integrated the Irish jig from early Irish immigrants. Tap dancing is all about tapping, clapping and snapping – using your body as a percussion instrument. Even chair-bound clients can do a modified form of tap if you place a square of MDF wooden board beneath their feet. Or, if a participant is unable to use their feet or snap their fingers, try an alternative like slapping the thighs instead or tapping the beat with a rhythm stick. Keep the tapping steps as simple as possible for those with dementia. Tap dancing without music, just tapping the feet to accentuate changes in rhythm, suits participants best as less background noise makes it easier to concentrate.

Charleston

The Charleston is also a favourite. Like the American tap, the Charleston was created by the African-American communities, and it became popular in the 1920s. Western women who danced the Charleston were known as 'flappers' and wore daring short skirts and bobbed their hair. The basic move is a kicking movement and the types of hand and leg movements required for the Charleston make it easily adapted for seated participants. I include a Charleston for seated clients in Part 3.

Ethnic dances

Since Britain is now one of the most ethnically diverse countries in the world, it is important that health care professionals embrace this and ensure that the histories, cultures and beliefs of minority ethnic populations are reflected in the activities we provide in care settings. According to Nat Lievesley's report, 'The Future Ageing of the Ethnic Minority Population of England and Wales', in 2051 in England and Wales, there will be 3.8 million black and minority ethnic people aged 65 and over, and 2.8 million aged 70 and over. Furthermore, between 2001 and 2051, there will be a 45-fold increase in the number of people living with dementia in the black African ethnic minority community (Lievesley 2010). As someone who is passionate about dance, movement and exercise, I feel that we must include all the cultures of the world in our work, not only for the benefit of the ethnic groups themselves but also for the positive contribution they make to the culture of the country as a whole. Right now, London, Birmingham, Leicester, Manchester and Liverpool have large immigrant populations, and some of my colleagues are introducing activities celebrating first-generation immigrants, by marking religious festivals and by inviting ethnic minority dancing and singing groups to perform and interact with all the residents.

We also have a range of European nationalities to cater for, many of whom have lived in Britain for a long time, and it is interesting for everyone to see their cultures represented in our work too.

Most people enjoy cultural diversity: staff, volunteers, carers and students on placements are keen to participate as part of their own learning curve. Although we have a very few older immigrants in nursing and residential homes in my local area of Dorset, we still celebrate different festivals because so many residents are knowledgeable about the contribution of Commonwealth countries to the history of this country – and especially enjoy the Commonwealth's contribution to the British diet.

Although we like to pin down ethnic dances to a particular country, often traditional dances cross national borders. Belly dancing, characteristic of both Middle Eastern and South East Asian traditional dances, is a prime example of this. Often, only the costume denotes the difference. Wherever they come from, the movements are an authentic expression of customs and beliefs and can be therapeutic as well as often being sacred in origin. Some dances are performed only on special occasions or for religious festivals; they may be ceremonial in nature, or they may mark life's milestones, like the transition from childhood to adulthood. Ethnic dances are also a rich source of variety in terms of props and percussion instruments (but beware: even simple moves can appear complicated when accompanied by a set of gongs or bamboo xylophones). Here are some examples:

- Indian dances can be adapted to chair-based exercises. While there are movements that imitate snakes, monkeys and tigers, there are also easier to follow moves for the fingers, head and eyes. Bollywood dance has become popular in recent years; it is often performed in community centres and is sometimes taught in schools.

- African dances are guaranteed to energise participants because of the tempo. African dances also come with a variety of musical instruments and props that will help with motivation. Just as the African continent is diverse, so is the range of dances: there are dances for women only, for men only, for boys in transition to manhood as well as for girls who are of marriageable age. The costumes can be as colourful as the props.

- Afro-Caribbean dancing has many African influences. Dancing and singing often accompany each other. I have tried reggae many times with great success. Reggae became popular in the 1960s after the arrival in Britain of Afro-Caribbean immigrants. The beat is pronounced and the tempo is very appealing to older people with disabilities. From experience, I know participants love to dance to Harry Belafonte's 'Day-O' and 'Island in the Sun'. The lyrics are clear and can easily be interpreted in BSL, Makaton, your own dance or movement interpretation or even in mime. I have also created various moves using straw/buri hats and brightly coloured fruits made of papier-mâché glued inside a bowl-like container to suggest the products of the Caribbean. Residents who are able to do 'turban movements' (different ways of folding and using the Afro-Caribbean scarves) should be encouraged to perform this exercise to maintain finger flexibility as well as for mental well-being. Sugar cane is a staple product from the Caribbean and I have often included a series of movements using foam tubes to represent sugar cane as a prop to accentuate stretching movements.

- Belly dancing is a dance worth persevering with, due to its popularity. Use walking frames to help with confidence because the key movement of belly dancing is shifting the weight from one foot to the other, and this is great for strengthening co-ordination and balance. For seated participants, shifting their weight from one buttock to another can be effective for balance and co-ordination and also activates their stomach muscles. Music is often evocative and the props can be colourful and tactile.

- Polynesian dances share characteristics with all the neighbouring islands of the South Pacific (Papua New Guinea, Samoa, Tonga and New Zealand) and percussion instruments from the Pacific islands are diverse and very stimulating, often having a trance-like effect on both participants and audience. Some of their percussion instruments can be made by residents and volunteers.

- South East Asian dancing can be both fast or slow. Most of the dance moves are gestures and therefore very expressive in character. There are so many interesting moves that older people have done in my sessions – especially for dances from the Philippines. Their history has left many cultural influences in music and dance: the Philippines were colonised by Spain and Japan, but have been heavily influenced by the US and the Middle East as a result of trading and military and religious activities. The southern islands are very Middle Eastern in style, sharing similarities with their Asian neighbours, which is reflected in the music and musical instruments. The northern islands are very European: 400 years as a Spanish colony have left their mark on the traditional dances there. I can highly recommend Asian movements for older people as they are easy to execute and there are many more slow tempo options that suit the elderly and disabled. Part 3 includes an example of an Oriental eye exercise.

Ballroom dancing

The popularity of ballroom dancing has enjoyed a huge revival in recent years, due in no small part to the success of various films and television programmes. This has motivated older people to take it up again. Tea dances are popular in residential homes as a social activity and organisations involved with the welfare of older people are running activities along these lines in the community to help older people to keep fit and maintain their independence. It is not easy to adapt ballroom dances to the frail elderly and chair-bound clients because ballroom dances are partner dances. Those who are able to stand and do the simple steps should be encouraged to do as much as they can. The music reminds older people of their active days, but you must concentrate on one dance at a time to avoid participants becoming confused. The waltz is a good place to start with its 3/4 tempo and relatively simple steps; there are instructions in Part 3.

Remember too that ballroom dancing is a great starting point for reminiscence work. Nearly all residents remember Fred and Ginger and their grace, elegance and romance that lifted the gloom in an era of depression.

The Can Can

The Can Can is a high energy dance. Women wear long, frilly petticoats and black stockings and the movements consist of lots of petticoat swishing, high kicks, lifting of skirts and flashing of underwear. Male dancers perform cartwheels, splits and tumbles. This exuberant dance promotes a sense of celebration and you can make simple props to add to the gaiety. You wouldn't think that such a high-spirited dance could be performed by chair-bound people, but I assure you that it can! Instructions for a Can Can adapted for seated dancers, choreographed by my colleagues in Dance Doctors, are included in Part 3.

Meditative exercises/dance movement

- T'ai Chi is a martial arts discipline traceable back to sixteenth-century China. It is often repetitive and slow but the therapeutic effect on both mental and physical health has long been recognised. Various studies of T'ai Chi by Arthritis Care provide compelling evidence of this. T'ai Chi promotes calmness and clarity of concentration. The aesthetic appeal comes from the graceful meditative moves of the body and it helps in maintaining homeostasis as well as circulation through the slow repetitions and breathing exercises. It is often referred to as 'meditation in motion'. Such is the popularity of T'ai Chi that many courses and sessions are now offered in day care centres, residential and nursing homes and in hospitals and rehabilitation centres. The centring effects of the movements help participants to cope with everyday stresses and even more so if you can perform outdoors where fresh air adds to the benefits and enjoyment.

- Qigong is a discipline which is similar to T'ai Chi, with its focus on meditation, concentration, awareness and moving gently. Qigong emphasises breathing techniques and stillness; if you can integrate breathing exercises and stillness into your sessions it will induce relaxation and lower anxiety levels in people suffering from mental health problems. Some movements concentrate on body-tapping, which improves circulation and stimulates the muscles. Qigong can be performed standing, sitting or lying down. Even those who are bed-bound and can only move a little can practise Qigong in one-to-one sessions. You do need to have some training before embarking on Qigong and many adult education organisations offer courses.

Action songs using sign language and Makaton

I worked with the Royal National Institute for Deaf People in Bath for 15 years and I thoroughly recommend this type of movement activity because sign language movements have no contraindications; all the movements are natural. You can work with the songs that participants can still remember from childhood – and this is true even for those in the advanced stages of dementia. You do need some knowledge of sign language (for sources of classes see Chapter 3). BSL is the language used by the deaf community and Makaton is a communication aid for people with learning difficulties, especially for those who cannot speak at all or who cannot speak clearly. Makaton was devised by speech therapist Margaret Walker and two hospital visitors from the Royal Association for Deaf people, Katherine Johnston and Tony Cornforth. The first two letters, 'ma', stand for Margaret, 'ka' for Katherine and 'ton' for Tony. Makaton signing is based on BSL but uses actions, speech and facial expression too. It means that you can use the most obvious and instinctive movement to convey meaning: for example, to describe a rainbow you raise one arm and draw an imaginary semicircle in the air.

Using sign language in dances is beneficial not only for people who are deaf and familiar with sign language; it is good for all elderly people to illustrate concepts visually for themselves and to communicate with others.

When you are devising actions to go with lyrics, pick out the key words in the poem or song you are signing for – don't try to interpret word for word, as you want your movements to fit the phrasing. Musicals, favourite hymns and Christmas carols can all be in interpreted in BSL and Makaton. In Part 3, I include a Makaton version of 'Morning Has Broken', but these are some tried and tested suggestions you might use.

From the musicals

Musicals from film and stage are very popular with older people. Here are some of the most popular musicals and songs which I have interpreted using BSL and Makaton during music and movement sessions:

'Oh What a Beautiful Morning!' from *Oklahoma*

'I'm Gonna Wash that Man right out of My Hair' from *South Pacific*

'Some Enchanted Evening' from *South Pacific*

'Getting to Know You' from *The King and I*

'Shall We Dance?' from *The King and I*

'Over the Rainbow' from *The Wizard of Oz*

'I'm Always Chasing Rainbows' from *Ziegfeld Girl*

'If I Loved You' from *Carousel*

'You'll Never Walk Alone' from *Carousel*

'Get Me to the Church on Time' from *My Fair Lady*

'I Could Have Danced All Night' from *My Fair Lady*

'Any Dream Will Do' from *Joseph and the Amazing Technicolour Dreamcoat*

'Black Hills of Dakota' from *Calamity Jane*

'Secret Love' from *Calamity Jane*

'Music of the Night' from *Phantom of the Opera*

'Consider Yourself' from *Oliver!*

'Where Is Love?' from *Oliver!*

'Good Morning' from *Singin' in the Rain*

'Singin' in the Rain' from *Singin' in the Rain.*

Favourite hymns

'Morning Has Broken' (see Part 3 for full instructions)

'Lord of the Dance'

'Rock of Ages'

Christmas carols

Singing and dancing using Christmas carols as the basis of your dance-based movement sessions will help participants embrace the spirit of Christmas and provide a rich resource for reminiscence work. Ensure that you start the session with something lyrical and simple to help build confidence. Always praise participants between each phase of the dance as they master the movements. The following Christmas carols are well loved and we have found them simple to work with:

'Silent Night, Holy Night'

'O Little Town of Bethlehem'

'Little Donkey'

'O Come All Ye Faithful'.

Sea shanties and songs about the sea

My interest in sea songs and shanties started in 1998 when I was working in a day centre. We had two retired fishermen in the group. One day they started to sing in their gravelly voices and told us about their experiences of the sea. The word 'shanty' comes from the French word '*chanter*', meaning to sing, and sea shanties were common in Europe, Australia, America and Britain (see Hughill 1961). The sea shanty was known as the sailor's work song in the days when things were done by muscle power rather than horse power. To get everyone to work in unison, a lead singer, called a shanty man, would sing his instructions and the rest of the men would join in with the chorus. By establishing and maintaining a rhythm in this way, sailors could maximise the muscle power of the crew. The lyrics tend to be repetitive; this works well for people with short memory spans and makes it easier for them to gain the satisfaction of mastering a song.

I collect anything to do with sea songs and shanties and more recently have added some old pirates' songs. Making props such as fishing nets decorated with handmade fish, mermaids, starfish and seaweed handmade from fabric and sewn on, collecting sea-smoothed shells and recreating old pirate maps have led to many interesting discussions in my sessions. Now I make sure I include sea songs and shanties, poems and verses in sessions I run during the summer; these lend themselves to intrepretation in BSL, Makaton, mime, dance and movement too. In Part 3 you will find a selection of sea songs and shanties.

Poetry

Older people love poetry and poems they may have learned by rote as children stay with them, word for word (see collections edited by Cotterell 1989 and Palgrave 1950). In 2000, a resident of Broadwindsor House surprised me when she recited John Masefield's poem, 'Sea Fever'. Not only did she remember every word, but she was also able to match her words with appropriate movements. It turned out that she could remember every poem she learned at school. Her favourite was William Wordsworth's 'I Wandered Lonely as a Cloud', and this inspired me to bring daffodils along to the next session so that residents could use them to improvise movements illustrating the images presented in this beautiful poem. Since then I have used poetry often as the starting point for dance and movement sessions, delighted to find that even clients in the first and middles stages of dementia respond to it. It helps to use background sound effects if they match the subject (e.g. recorded sounds of the ocean for a sea poem), or music can add to the mood or atmosphere a poem creates (for a religious poem, I would play religious music, perhaps a hymn without any lyrics).

I find these poems go down particularly well:

'Sea Fever' by John Masefield

'Night Mail' by W.H. Auden

'Trees' by Alfred Joyce Kilmer

'The Tyger' by William Blake

'I Wandered Lonely as a Cloud' by William Wordsworth.

Don't be over-ambitious in trying to teach the whole poem at once. Concentrate on one stanza at a time so that participants can enjoy achieving mastery of the movements before they are challenged again.

Dances by theme

Holidays and festivals are a good source of themes around which you can create dance and movement sessions and make links with other activities like reminiscence work, arts and crafts activities, and group discussions. In Appendix 1 you will find a list of special days, celebrations and festivals. I have found the following themes offer plenty of scope:

- Chinese New Year (falls on a date during late January to mid-February depending on the moon). There are many styles of Chinese dance which can be adapted for active, less able, and chair-bound participants. As well as a wide range of music to choose from, you can add props like fans, ribbons and Chinese lanterns, wind chimes and bells. You could make up a wall display of Chinese symbols and examples of Chinese brocades which you can buy in fabric shops or from car boot sales. As an art project you could make a papier-mâché dragon or perhaps the animal representing the new year (rat, ox, tiger, rabbit, dragon, snake, horse, etc.).

- Commonwealth Day (second Monday in March). Consider running a dance session focusing on Indian dances and movements, which are particularly good for maintaining mobility in the wrists and fingers. Dances can be either slow and reflective or lively. There is an abundance of music and props to choose from. Some samples of cotton and silk sari fabrics, with their jewel-like colours, will appeal to participants and wrapping the sari around the body is a useful exercise in itself. You could also incorporate some African dances; these work well as the rhythms are strong and compelling, provoking participants to move. Find or make a range of unusual percussion instruments and let each participant choose one to add their own sound to the music.

- United Nations Day (24 October). This is ideal for flag dances. You can use the flags of the country of origin of participants or of countries participants have visited. Flags are useful for hand and arm exercises; make sure particular care is taken with the sticks. I find there is never a dull moment once participants are holding a flag!

- Grandparents' Day (first Sunday after US Labor Day, which is the first Monday in September). As many residents in residential and nursing homes are grandparents, this is a day already ringed on the calendar. On this Sunday, visitors are often expected, so you could prepare a session that uses movement to interpret a poem about grandparents or prepare and lead some dances that visitors can join in with.

- Mad Hatter's Day (10 June in Britain). This can be very colourful and great fun. You could decorate a collection of hats for the occasion. Songs from the musicals lend themselves to dances with hats as props and you could combine movements with hats with movements with walking sticks for the more active class.

- International Dance Day (29 April). For this day you could use a selection of any of the international dances suggested throughout this book.

10

A Note About Wheelchair Dancing

Wheelchair dancing is understandably not for the frail elderly unless they can be partnered by a carer, relative or volunteer to push them. The room must be spacious to avoid accidents.

Wheelchair dancing is often referred to as 'dancing on wheels'. It has the same health benefits as any other physical activity. It can be a social and recreational activity. It has also become a competitive sport called 'wheelchair dance sport' and as such is governed by the International Paralympic Committee. It can be very challenging for participants, both disabled and non-disabled, because it takes time and energy to synchronise with each other.

There are different types of wheelchair dancing:

- Individual or solo dance, which is usually freestyle.

- Duo dance is a dance for two wheelchair users. The movements of the dancers must be performed in unison or mirroring each other.

- Partner/combination dance is a dance partnership between a disabled and a non-disabled person.

- Team dance is performed by a group of wheelchair users. The number in the group dictates which dance style is performed. Formation or sequence dancing are both popular group dances.

Dances you can adapt for wheelchair users include ballroom dancing, line dancing, formation dancing, some ethnic dances and freestyle dancing.

Wheelchair dance has been celebrated on BBC television, not only in programmes but also in the signature footage between programmes.

Wheelchair dancing is recommended for young adults who have limited or no movement in the lower part of the body. Anyone interested in running a music and movement session should do some training in wheelchair dancing with specialists like the Candoco Dance Company. There is nothing that can improve your knowledge of dance and movement more than having the experience of performing the moves yourself.

Part 3

THE DANCES

The Dances

Lively Dances

Dances from Far Away

Sea Shanties and Songs About the Sea

Dances Popular in the Twentieth Century

11

Warm-up

Choreography: Petra Hughes

Introduction: It is essential to gently warm up the limbs, joints and muscles before beginning any of the structured dances. A good plan for a warm-up sequence is to start by making small, limited movements in response to a cheerful music track and then to repeat all the movements, this time slightly increasing the range of each movement, and so on. Below are some of the elements of a warm-up with which you can create your own warm-up routine.

Performed: standing or seated.

Suitable for: the opening of a session.

Will help with: preparing the body for a session of dance and movement to music, setting the tone.

Watch out for: breathing too shallowly on the out-breath, which can lead to hyperventilating. Also look out for too wide a range of each movement from the start; better to start with a small version of each movement and then build up its range slightly each time the basic routine is repeated. Don't move too swiftly from one movement to the next: make sure everybody has got it before bringing in a new movement – up to a maximum of 16 counts is good. Make sure everybody can see you to follow you as you demonstrate each movement.

Music: Something cheerful and with a clear, easily identified rhythm, such as 'Raindrops Keep Falling on My Head'. Alternatively something percussive and joyful such as 'So Lonely' by Marcus Corbett or a recording of gentle chants from Tibetan monks.

Props: (Optional) Cushions to help feet remain flat on the floor.

Movements

Preparation	Sit up tall, feet hip-width apart. Breathe in slowly, then breathe out slowly (for the same count as in-breath). Be aware of all your muscles and let them relax while you concentrate on your breathing. Encourage being in the moment and letting worries go.
Breathing	Breathe in slowly and deeply and as you do so lower your arms and scoop air towards your mouth. Breathe out to the same count and as you do so, with palms facing down, press air down to the ground. Rotate palms.
Shoulders	Lift and drop then roll shoulders backwards slowly, then forwards. One at a time, then both together.
Arms	Use opening, lifting, lowering, scooping and circling movements that can start small, i.e. from the elbow, and build up to movements from the shoulder.
Wrists	Circle the wrists. Turn palms during the course of an arm movement.

Hands and fingers	Rub hands together, wring them and clap. Wriggle fingers and thumbs as if rippling through water.
Waist and stomach	Sway from side to side.
Lower legs and ankles	Lift the heel of each foot in turn. Flex each foot in turn, i.e. digging heel in, lifting toe. Circle each foot in turn, keeping the toes in contact with the ground.
Feet	Lift toes, tap feet. Build up to light stamps and lower leg lifts.
Circulation	Rub arms and legs with hands. Mark rhythm by patting thighs and knees.

12

'My Bonnie Lies Over the Ocean' (Bath-time)

Everyday Activities

Choreography: Delia Silvester

Introduction: This is a good example of the way that exercise can be non-invasive through the use of movements that people are already familiar with and have performed throughout their lives. It turns everyday gestures into a simple yet delightful movement sequence. 'My Bonnie Lies Over the Ocean' is a well-known song and you can use the chorus to repeat the arms sequence to help people get used to the movements. When you are familiar with the whole sequence, you may find that you can use it with different songs.

Performed: seated.

Suitable for: creating a gentle and playful mood. Good for a warm-up.

Will help with: reminiscence work around daily lives and self-nourishment. People in residential homes are usually touched only when staff are attending to their physical needs. They are not touched playfully, or tenderly, or sensuously; it would not be appropriate for staff to touch them in such a way. This sequence gives them a chance to touch their own bodies in a playful and affectionate way. Holding and manipulating the sponges throughout the dance helps with maintaining hand and wrist movement and manual control, although it can also be done with pretend sponges.

Watch out for: over-stretching. Make sure that everyone can see your movements and that you demonstrate them with enthusiasm to make it a really enjoyable experience.

Music: 'My Bonnie Lies Over the Ocean' is the song that we've set the movements to (below). There are various versions of this available online, some as free downloads; the words or the order of the verses may vary slightly, but as long as the version you choose has four verses and four choruses it will fit to the movements given below. You could also adapt the moves to 'I'm Forever Blowing Bubbles' (played through twice) or 'I'm in the Mood for Love'.

Props: Ideally everyone needs two small sponges, one for each hand, which they can pretend to wash themselves with. Otherwise, people can just pretend to hold sponges.

As a back-up activity: you could make your own basic bubble solution. This needs: 1/3 cup washing-up liquid or baby shampoo; 1/4 cup water; and 2 tsp. sugar. Combine the ingredients and pour into an unbreakable bottle. To blow bubbles, experiment using plastic straws or pipe cleaners.

Words

My Bonnie lies over the ocean,
My Bonnie lies over the sea,
My Bonnie lies over the ocean,
O bring back my Bonnie to me.

[Chorus]

Bring back, bring back,
Bring back my Bonnie to me, to me,
Bring back, bring back,
O bring back my Bonnie to me.

O blow, ye winds, over the ocean,
And blow, ye winds, over the sea,
O blow, ye winds, over the ocean,
And bring back my Bonnie to me.

[Chorus]

Last night as I lay on my pillow,
Last night as I lay on my bed,
Last night as I lay on my pillow,
I dreamed that my Bonnie was dead.

[Chorus]

The winds have blown over the ocean,
The winds have blown over the sea,
The winds have blown over the ocean,
And brought back my Bonnie to me.

Brought back, brought back,
Brought back my Bonnie to me, to me,
Brought back, brought back,
O brought back my Bonnie to me.

Lyrics: traditional Scottish folk song

Movements

You could introduce this with, 'We're all going to have a treat, pretending to soak in a luxurious bath and washing ourselves.'

The instruction says 'scrub', but since this is a dance it is more like stroking.

Verse one	
My Bonnie lies over the ocean,	Open hot tap.
My Bonnie lies over the sea,	Close hot tap.
My Bonnie lies over the ocean,	Open cold tap (with other hand).
O bring back my Bonnie to me.	Close cold tap (with other hand).
Chorus	
Bring back, bring back,	Scrub full length of right arm (front).
Bring back my Bonnie to me, to me,	Scrub full length of right arm (back).
Bring back, bring back,	Scrub full length of left arm (front).
O bring back my Bonnie to me.	Scrub full length of left arm (back).
Verse two	
O blow, ye winds, over the ocean,	Scrub right elbow in circles.
O blow, ye winds, over the sea,	Change direction of circles.

O blow, ye winds, over the ocean,	Scrub left elbow in circles.
And bring back my Bonnie to me.	Change direction of circles.
Chorus	
Bring back, bring back,	Scrub full length of right arm (front).
Bring back my Bonnie to me, to me,	Scrub full length of right arm (back).
Bring back, bring back,	Scrub full length of left arm (front).
O bring back my Bonnie to me.	Scrub full length of left arm (back).
Verse three	
Last night as I lay on my pillow,	Scrub right knee in circles.
Last night as I lay on my bed,	Change direction of circles.
Last night as I lay on my pillow,	Scrub left knee in circles.
I dreamed that my Bonnie was dead.	Change direction of circles.
Chorus	
Bring back, bring back,	Scrub full length of right arm (front).
Bring back my Bonnie to me, to me,	Scrub full length of right arm (back).

Bring back, bring back,	Scrub full length of left arm (front).
O bring back my Bonnie to me.	Scrub full length of left arm (back).
Verse four	
The winds have blown over the ocean,	Scrub outside of right thigh in long strokes.
The winds have blown over the sea,	Scrub inside of right thigh in long strokes.
The winds have blown over the ocean,	Scrub outside of left thigh in long strokes.
And brought back my Bonnie to me.	Scrub inside of left thigh in long strokes.
Chorus	
Brought back, brought back,	Scrub chest down to tummy in zig-zags.
Brought back my Bonnie to me, to me,	Scrub back up again from tummy to chest in zig-zags.
Brought back, brought back,	Rub hands together softly as if rinsing off the soap.
O brought back my Bonnie to me.	Hold arms reaching out wide in greeting/celebration.

13

'Dashing Away with the Smoothing Iron' (Laundry)

Everyday Activities

Choreography: Lucy Goodison and Petra Hughes

Introduction: This is a traditional folk song celebrating daily life, written in the nineteenth century. The movements are simple, copying the movements of household chores; doing the washing is something every participant will have been very familiar with.

Performed: seated.

Suitable for: groups not very used to dance sessions as the movements are not challenging.

Will help with: reminiscence work around daily lives.

Music: 'Dashing away with the Smoothing Iron' (various available).

Props: None needed as participants can do the movements with imaginary linen. Alternatively you can give everyone a clean, white handkerchief, or a white kitchen cloth of the type that can be bought cheaply in packs.

Words

VERSE ONE: MONDAY – WASHING

'Twas on a Monday morning
When I beheld my darling;
She looked so neat and charming
In every high degree;
She looked so neat and nimble, Oh,
A-washing of her linen, Oh,
Dashing away with the smoothing iron,
Dashing away with the smoothing iron,
She stole my heart away.

VERSE TWO: TUESDAY – HANGING

'Twas on a Tuesday morning
When I beheld my darling;
She looked so neat and charming
In every high degree;
She looked so neat and nimble, Oh,
A-hanging of her linen, Oh,
Dashing away with the smoothing iron,
Dashing away with the smoothing iron,
She stole my heart away.

VERSE THREE: WEDNESDAY – STARCHING

'Twas on a Wednesday morning
When I beheld my darling;
She looked so neat and charming
In every high degree;
She looked so neat and nimble, Oh,
A-starching of her linen, Oh,
Dashing away with the smoothing iron,
Dashing away with the smoothing iron,
She stole my heart away.

VERSE FOUR: THURSDAY – IRONING

'Twas on a Thursday morning
When I beheld my darling;
She looked so neat and charming
In every high degree;

She looked so neat and nimble, Oh,
A-ironing of her linen, Oh,
Dashing away with the smoothing iron,
Dashing away with the smoothing iron,
She stole my heart away.

VERSE FIVE: FRIDAY – FOLDING
'Twas on a Friday morning
When I beheld my darling;
She looked so neat and charming
In every high degree;
She looked so neat and nimble, Oh,
A-folding of her linen, Oh,
Dashing away with the smoothing iron,
Dashing away with the smoothing iron,
She stole my heart away.

VERSE SIX: SATURDAY – AIRING
'Twas on a Saturday morning
When I beheld my darling;
She looked so neat and charming
In every high degree;
She looked so neat and nimble, Oh,
A-airing of her linen, Oh,
Dashing away with the smoothing iron,
Dashing away with the smoothing iron,
She stole my heart away.

VERSE SEVEN: SUNDAY – WEARING
'Twas on a Sunday morning
When I beheld my darling;
She looked so neat and charming
In every high degree;
She looked so neat and nimble, Oh,
A-wearing of her linen, Oh,
Dashing away with the smoothing iron,
Dashing away with the smoothing iron,
She stole my heart away.

Lyrics: traditional

Movements

Verse one: Monday	
'Twas on a Monday morning	Open right arm from elbow, open left arm from elbow.
When I beheld my darling;	Place right arm to left shoulder, place left arm to right shoulder (arms across chest).
She looked so neat and charming	Cup left cheek with left hand, then right cheek with right hand.
In every high degree;	Keeping hands in place, sway from the waist rhythmically.
She looked so neat and nimble, Oh, *A-washing of her linen, Oh,*	Make plunging and washing movements.
Dashing away with the smoothing iron, Dashing away with the smoothing iron,	With right arm as if holding an iron, smooth across 'ironing board' right to left, repeat.
She stole my heart away.	Hands to heart and then open both arms out from the elbow.
Verse two: Tuesday	
'Twas on a Tuesday morning	Open right arm from elbow, open left arm from elbow.
When I beheld my darling;	Place right arm to left shoulder, place left arm to right shoulder.

She looked so neat and charming	Cup left cheek with left hand, then right cheek with right hand.
In every high degree;	Keeping hands in place, sway from the waist rhythmically.
She looked so neat and nimble, Oh, *A-hanging of her linen, Oh,*	Movements as if pegging linen on the line to dry.
Dashing away with the smoothing iron, Dashing away with the smoothing iron,	With left arm as if holding an iron, smooth across 'ironing board' left to right, repeat.
She stole my heart away.	Hands to heart and then open both arms out from the elbow.
Verse three: Wednesday	
She looked so neat and nimble, Oh, *A-starching of her linen, Oh,*	Movements as if splashing or spraying starch on to linen on ironing board.
Verse four: Thursday	
She looked so neat and nimble, Oh, *A-ironing of her linen, Oh,*	Movements as if ironing linen on an ironing board. Use alternate arms.
Verse five: Friday	
She looked so neat and nimble, Oh, *A-folding of her linen, Oh,*	Movements as if folding: palms down, pat right palm on top of left on the 'ironing board', remove left palm and pat on top of right and repeat.

Verse six: Saturday	
She looked so neat and nimble, Oh, *A-airing of her linen, Oh,*	Movements as if airing: lift folded linen up to the air to right side of face, then lift to left side of face.
Verse seven: Sunday	
She looked so neat and nimble, Oh, *A-wearing of her linen, Oh,*	Proudly smooth down length of right sleeve, then left sleeve, then smooth down front of 'dress'.

14

Greek Greeting Dance

Circle Dances

Choreography: traditional, introduced into the sacred/circle dance repertoire by Bernhard Wosien and annotated by Janet McCrickard in Dancing Circles *(1985)*

Introduction: This very simple dance from the Greek island of Kos is about participants greeting other participants on the opposite side of the circle and then moving back into their own space. It has been called 'the most ancient surviving European dance'.

Performed: standing or seated.

Suitable for: participants who can stand independently and for those confined to a seat. It suits a communal occasion and is ideal for the beginning of a session (greeting) or for the end of a session (leave-taking).

Will help with: promoting a sense of community through contact with each other. It also gently exercises the legs.

Watch out for: overstretching to reach a neighbour's hand, or leaning too far forward from a seated position. Also people who have had a hip replacement should not step too far to the side.

Music: the best piece of music for this dance is 'Enas Mythos' though any slow Greek music will do.

Props: None.

Movements

Hold hands in a circle throughout the dance (traditionally with crossed arms as in 'Auld Lang Syne', but that may be a stretch too far).

As the main elements are stepping and leaning forward, the dance can easily be adapted to suit seated participants. Seated participants should be encouraged to sit forward on the edge of their chair and, like standing participants, be able to hold hands with their neighbours in a comfortable, short stretch. Feet should be a little apart. It is a good idea to practise bouncing on the heels before starting; the bounce should be a very gentle one, the knees bend only slightly.

1. Left foot steps forward.

2. Right foot steps forward to join it.

3. Bounce (bend) the knees twice (if seated, bounce with heels).

4. Right foot steps back.

5. Left foot steps back to join it.

6. Bounce (bend) the knees twice (if seated, bounce with heels).

7. Right foot steps to the right.

8. Left foot joins it.

9. Bounce (bend) the knees twice (if seated, bounce with heels).

10. Left foot steps to the left.

11. Right foot joins it.

12. Bounce (bend) the knees twice (if seated, bounce with heels).

13. Repeat the whole sequence.

NB

If the group is standing, the movement to the right can be repeated several times so that the group moves round in the circle before stepping to the left and moving back again.

Janet McCrickard refers to an interpretation of this dance in which the step forward means 'I greet you', the step back means 'I give you space' while the sideways movement can represent the group flowing onward together (Harrison 1985, p.1).

15

Create Your Own Circle Dance

Circle Dances

Choreography: devised by Lucy Goodison

Introduction: Below are some of the basic elements of a circle dance. You can choose a piece of music to suit the participants and their mood, and then with these elements you can create a sequence of movements to suit their abilities. You can add complexity to the dance as they respond.

Performed: seated, or for participants who can stand independently and those who can stand holding on to a wheelchair, chair or walking frame.

Suitable for: creating a playful, collective mood.

Will help with: promoting collective sharing and community through contact with each other. It will also provide gentle exercise for arm and leg muscles.

Watch out for: participants who are a little wobbly; encourage them to use a stable chair or a walking frame to help their sense of balance and safety.

Music: You choose. Anything gentle and folksy – perhaps something used in a ceilidh if it is not too fast.

Props: You might choose a simple item of costume to add to the folk atmosphere.

Movements

Travelling steps (all of which can be done stationary in a chair)

- Step in line.

- Skip in line.

- Forward gallop, side gallop.

- Grapevine (left foot in front of right, right foot beside it, left foot behind right, right foot beside it; if seated, repeat the other way. This lovely step which brings a gentle hip swing is sadly not suitable for people with hip replacements.) With travelling steps, you can always circle one way then change direction.

Punctuation movements

- Step and close.

- Brush foot across in front (not for people with hip replacements).

- Bounce.

- Sway.

- Point foot in front and bring back.

- Raise knee and lower again.

- Hop with other knee raised (if seated).

- Swing joined arms back and forth.

- Kick lower leg out behind.

- Pat body.

- Clap hands.

Ways to link up

- Arms around waists.

- Hold hands.

- Hold hands with arms crossed in front.

- Join little fingers.

- Form a chain at shoulder height

Other elements

- Move into the middle and out.

- Face a partner and hold hands.

You can adapt the sequence you create to suit your group. For example, a seated group who are holding hands might enjoy a sequence consisting of:

- Swing joined arms × 4; sway × 4; skip on the spot × 4; then clap × 4. Repeat.

Alternatively, a standing group steadying themselves on walking frames might enjoy a sequence consisting of:

- Raise knee, raise other knee, step to right and close; raise knee, raise other knee, step to left and close; pat body × 4; sway × 4. Repeat.

A standing and mobile group, on the other hand, could perhaps put arms round waists and include some travelling steps that actually travel.

The secret is to repeat the sequence until people know it well enough to relax and enjoy sharing the movements with their group.

16

Morris Dance with Sticks

Folk Dances and Songs

Choreography: Petra Hughes and Lucy Goodison

Introduction: This dance focuses on rhythm and percussion. Ideally, participants need to be able to face each other in pairs to knock 'sticks', but the dance can also be done with people seated in a line or in a circle (see below).

Performed: seated or standing.

Suitable for: springtime and for a mix of abilities. Also useful for reminiscence work, especially around childhood and memories of May Day festivities, and is particularly suited to rural communities.

Will help with: raising energy levels and communication. Knocking the sticks also allows space for the playful and safe expression of feelings.

Watch out for: participants missing the stick and hitting each other; however, using the props suggested, they won't hurt each other. It is a good idea for participants to practise the rhythm both with feet and 'sticks' before trying it out with the music.

Music: 'The Duke of York's Troope', Sharon Shannon, *Out the Gap*, The Daisy Label (2007).

Props: For the 'sticks', use foam pipe insulation available from plumbing suppliers, and cut to lengths of about three feet. The insulation tubing tends to be grey in colour and so the sticks can be decorated with coloured sticky tape to make them more visible and more fun. You could place footboards made of squares of MDF or linoleum under the feet for seated clients.

Extra activities: You could make paper flowers and attach them to soft hats or bowler-type hats to wear while doing this dance, in the style of many morris dancers. Alternatively bells attached to ribbons and tied round the ankles can add an extra dimension of sound to the foot stamping (beware sharp edges).

Words: None.

Movements

This dance focuses on rhythm. During the 'verses' the rhythm is marked out by feet; during the 'breaks' the rhythm is marked out by participants knocking each other's sticks. It may take two or three sessions to learn this dance.

Rhythm for the 'verses'

- **Right**-left-right (hop on right, or lift right leg), **left**-right-left (hop on left, or lift left leg), **right, left, right, left.**

- **Right**-left-right (hop on right, or lift right leg), **left**-right-left (hop on left, or lift left leg), **right, left, right** and close.

Seated participants can make the skipping movements with their lower legs from a chair or wheelchair. If they cannot do that, then they can mark out the rhythm by tapping their heels or tapping their toes. If no leg movement is possible, the rhythm can be marked by tapping the thigh with a hand. Standing participants may not be able to hop but they can follow the same rhythm and just hold the foot still for a beat instead of hopping, that is, **right**-left-right (hold one count with weight on right), **left**-right-left (hold one count with weight on left), and so on.

Rhythm for the 'breaks', knocking sticks

- **Knock**-knock-knock, **knock**-knock-knock, **knock, knock, knock, knock** (now swap who makes the knock and who receives it).

- **Knock**-knock-knock, **knock**-knock-knock, **knock, knock, knock, knock**.

If participants are able to sit or stand facing each other in pairs, the rhythm can be marked out by knocking on the stick of a partner opposite them; at the end of each line, swap who makes the knock and who holds the stick to receive the knock.

If seated in a line or circle, participants can turn first to knock sticks with the person on their right, and then at the next break, with the person on the left. Alternatively, a mobile person could knock sticks with a person in a wheelchair facing them. If knocking sticks with someone else is not possible, the stick can be used to mark out the rhythm on the chair arm, the floor or the shoulder.

Whether standing or seated, participants should be encouraged to change the arm holding the stick so that both arms get equal exercise.

17

Morris Dance with Hankies

Folk Dances and Songs

Choreography: Petra Hughes and Lucy Goodison

Introduction: Many participants will be familiar with morris dancing and associate it with spring.

Performed: standing or seated.

Suitable for: springtime, especially May. Also useful for reminiscence work especially around childhood and memories of May Day festivities, and is particularly suited to rural communities.

Will help with: exercising and maintaining hand and wrist flexibility in participants who may not have much strength there.

Watch out for: In the instructions, a 'high' shake of the hankies means only as high as participants can safely reach, which will probably not be above shoulder height. A 'low' shake for standing participants does not involve bending, but for seated participants may involve them bending forward to shake hankies on either side of their knees; or it may mean participants remaining seated with back straight and shaking hankies over the side of their chair arms on either side. Take care that seated participants do not bend further forward than is safe for them on this low hanky shake. It is a good idea to practise with participants first to make sure that they know what their limits are. For seated version: if participants cannot skip with their feet, they can lift their heels in time with the beat; if they can't do that, they can lift their toes in time, whilst lifting the hankies as described.

Music: 'Padstow', Steeleye Span, *Tempted and Tried*, [CD] Music Digital (2003).

Props: Two white hankies for each person.

Extra activities: You could make paper flowers and attach them to soft hats to wear while doing this dance, in the style of many morris dancers. Alternatively bells attached to ribbons and tied round the wrists can add an extra dimension of sound to the movements (beware sharp edges).

Words

Unite and unite, and let us all unite
For summer is a-comin' today
And whither we are going we all will unite
In the merry morning of May.

The young men of Padstow they might if they would
For summer is a-comin' today
They might have built a ship and gilded it with gold
In the merry morning of May.

The young maids of Padstow they might if they would
For summer is a-comin' today
They might have built a garland with the white rose and the red
In the merry morning of May.

Rise up, Mrs Johnson, all in your gown of green
For summer is a-comin' today
You are as fine a lady as waits upon the Queen
In the merry morning of May.

Oh where is King George, oh where is he-o?
He's out in his longboat, all on the salt sea-o
Up flies the kite, down falls the lark-o
Aunt Ursula Birdon she had an old ewe
And she died in her own park-o.

With the merry ring and with the joyful spring
For summer is a-comin' today
How happy are the little birds and the merrier we shall sing
In the merry morning of May.

Oh where are the young men that now do advance?
For summer is a-comin' today
Oh some they are in England and some they are in France
In the merry morning of May.

Lyrics: traditional

Movements

(Musical introduction)	Hold one hanky in each hand, shake them gently to the front and look to right and left towards neighbours. Then circle wrists in front.
Verse one	
Unite and unite, and	Shake hankies to the right, low.
let us all unite	Shake hankies to the right, high.
For summer is a-comin' today	Shake hankies to the left, low.
And whither we	Shake hankies to the left, high.
are going we all will unite	Shake hankies to the right, low.
In the merry	Shake hankies to the right, high.
morning of May.	Shake hankies to the left, low then high.
Verse two	
The young men of Padstow they might if they would *For summer is a-comin' today* *They might have built a ship and gilded it with gold* *In the merry morning of May.*	Throughout the verse, swing each arm up in turn with the hankies and make skipping movements with the feet. Repeat throughout verse.
Verse three	
The young maids of Padstow	Shake hankies to the right, low.

they might if they would	Shake hankies to the right, high.
For summer is a-comin'	Shake hankies to the left, low.
today	Shake hankies to the left, high.
They might have built a garland with the white rose and the	Shake hankies to the right, low.
red	Shake hankies to the right, high.
In the merry morning of May.	Shake hankies to the left, low then high.
Verse four	
Rise up, Mrs Johnson, all in your gown of green *For summer is a-comin' today* *You are as fine a lady as waits upon the Queen* *In the merry morning of May.*	Throughout the verse, swing both arms up and down together and make skipping movements with the feet. Repeat throughout verse.
Verse five	
Oh where is King George, oh where is he-o?	Shake hankies gently to front below hands.
He's out in his longboat, all on the salt sea-o	Move hands as if rowing.
Up flies the kite, down falls the lark-o *Aunt Ursula Birdon she had an old ewe* *And she died in her own park-o.*	Flip right hanky up across body and over left shoulder then slowly stroke it down. Repeat with alternate hands.

Verse six	
With the merry ring and	Shake hankies to the right, low.
with the joyful spring	Shake hankies to the right, high.
For summer is a-comin'	Shake hankies to the left, low.
today	Shake hankies to the left, high.
How happy are the little birds and the merrier we shall	Shake hankies to the right, low.
sing	Shake hankies to the right, high.
In the merry morning of May.	Shake hankies to the left, low then high.
Verse seven	
Oh where are the young men that now do advance? For summer is a-comin' today Oh some they are in England and some they are in France In the merry morning of May.	Throughout the verse, swing hankies together across body and out and make skipping movements with the feet. Repeat throughout verse.
	End by all raising hankies together.

18

'Oats and Beans and Barley Grow'

Folk Dances and Songs

Choreography: Lucy Goodison and Petra Hughes

Introduction: This is a traditional British and American folk song that can be dated back to the nineteenth century. Participants may remember singing it in the playground.

Performed: seated or standing.

Suitable for: reminiscence work especially around childhood, and is particularly suited to rural communities.

Will help with: maintaining mobility in the hands.

Watch out for: raising the hands too high.

Music: 'Oats and Beans and Barley Grow', Frank McConnell, [MP3 download] Classic Fox Records, (2000).

Props: None.

Extra activities: Reminiscence and discussion about growing vegetables or farm work.

Words

Oats and beans and barley grow
Oats and beans and barley grow
Not you nor I nor anyone knows
How oats and beans and barley grow.

First the farmer plants his seeds
Then he stands and takes his ease
Stamps his feet and claps his hands
And turns around to view his lands.

Oats and beans and barley grow
Oats and beans and barley grow
Not you nor I nor anyone knows
How oats and beans and barley grow.

Lyrics: traditional

NB

Some people like to add more verses, replacing the word 'plants' his seeds with 'waters' his seeds and 'hoes' his weeds, which extends the song and invites the invention of more actions to match. In some versions the farmer has become a 'she'.

Movements

Verse one	
Oats and beans and barley grow *Oats and beans and barley grow*	Hold hands up at chest height in front with fingers pointing up, wiggle fingers and lift hands slowly to convey growth × 2.
Not you nor I nor anyone knows	Point to another, point to self then slide hands horizontally to indicate 'no one'.
How oats and beans and barley grow.	Repeat actions from first line.
Verse two	
First the farmer plants his seeds	Invert fist with thumb out pointing down and push down as if pushing seed into soil.
Then he stands and takes his ease	Fold arms.
Stamps his feet and claps his hands	Stamp feet. Clap hands.
And turns around to view his lands.	Look to the side or both sides.
Verse three	
Oats and beans and barley grow *Oats and beans and barley grow*	Hold hands up at chest height in front with fingers pointing up, wiggle fingers and lift hands slowly to convey growth × 2.

Not you nor I nor anyone knows	Point to another, point to self then slide hands horizontally to indicate 'no one'.
How oats and beans and barley grow.	Repeat actions from first line.

19

'Amazing Grace'

Spiritual

Choreography: Lucy Goodison and Petra Hughes

Introduction: This is a sacred dance and the words have been adapted to suit older participants. It connects participants to their life experiences – even sad ones.

Performed: standing or seated.

Suitable for: serious moments when the atmosphere is calm. It could provide a familiar ritual for closing – or opening – every movement session.

Will help with: perpetuating a calm mood and promoting sensitivity. Simple movements enable participants to experience body awareness through touching their bodies and to promote a sense of community through holding hands and eye contact with others.

Watch out for: over-stretching, especially above shoulders where contraindicated, and jerky movements. It is a good idea to practise singing the song first separately before introducing the movements.

Music: 'Amazing Grace' (any slow version, *without* lyrics) – or the adapted words (below) can be sung without any music.

Props: None.

Words

Amazing Grace
How sweet the sound
That saved a soul
Like me.
I've loved and lost
But I'm still here
And holding hands
With thee.

Lyrics: John Newton (1779), here adapted

Movements

You might introduce the dance by saying that some believe the soul lies in the belly, while the midriff is the site of the more selfish 'me, me, me'. The heart is to do with loving, and when we empty our hands in the song it signifies letting go; we have all had to let go of things along the way. When we pat our thighs in the dance we are saying, 'Look, my legs root me to the earth and I'm still here!' When we reach to the side in the dance we are reaching for contact with others and for a sense of community which we all need.

This dance utilises the 'hark' movement: cupping the hands to the ears as if listening.

Amazing Grace	Scoop up with arms and lift into an arch above head if possible, then open out to shoulder height.
How sweet the sound	Bring elbows into side, make 'hark' gesture with right hand and swivel from the waist to the right.
That saved a soul	Place right hand on belly.
Like me.	Place left hand on midriff.
I've loved	Place both hands on heart.
and lost	Empty the hands downwards as if dropping something.
But I'm still here	Bring hands to thighs and pat thighs on the words 'I'm', 'still' and 'here'.
And holding hands	Reach out to the side to join hands with person on each side.
With thee.	Eye contact with people on either side.

20

'Step Softly on the Earth'

Spiritual

Choreography: Petra Hughes and Lucy Goodison

Introduction: This draws inspiration from the four elements of earth, air, fire and water; from Native American sacred dancing; and from a song by Carolyn Hillyer, composer and singer of sacred songs. It is performed in a circle.

Performed: standing or seated in a circle.

Suitable for: performing early in a session when there is a quiet, relaxed mood, or at the close to give a familiar and meditative ending.

Will help with: perpetuating a calm, relaxed mood and promoting sensitivity. This simple sequence encourages subtlety of movement, using visualisation and the natural world. It promotes breathing and the gentle use of arms and legs, as well as imagination.

Watch out for: breathing. It is important that in-breaths are matched by equally long out-breaths to avoid hyperventilating.

Music: You could choose background music with a Native American flavour, create your own or do the movements without music and simply chant the words in a sing-song pattern that fits the mood.

Props: (Optional) Something Native American like a headband and/or a fabric feather.

Extra activities: You could make simple Native American headbands with scarves or ribbons (avoid real feathers).

Words

Step softly on the Earth
Breathe lightly of the air
Dance brightly like the fire flames
Rest gently on the waves.

Lyrics: Lucy Goodison and Petra Hughes

Movements

If standing, form a circle, sides to the middle facing clockwise, hands at elbow or hip height parallel to the floor. Bounce as if feeling the energy of the earth in Native American style around a campfire. Start with some breathing exercises. If the group is seated in a circle, the walking movements can be done on the spot in a chair.

Step softly on the Earth	Walk forwards, gently stamping with a bouncy step × 4.
Breathe lightly of the air	Turn to face the middle of the circle and open arms to make light scooping movements and breathe in and out.
Dance brightly like the fire flames	Elbows by your sides, lift hands and wiggle them with fingers and thumbs like flickering flames.
Rest gently on the waves.	With both hands forward, palms down, make gentle wave-like movements from side to side.

21

'Morning Has Broken'

Spiritual

Choreography: Delia Silvester

Introduction: This is a popular Christian hymn and familiar to most people. In this version, some elements of sign language are used. You may feel a bit daunted when you first try this dance as there appear to be so many movements, but don't be put off; the movements are actually very simple and repetitive. Watch the demonstration of the dance online (http://www.jkp.com/catalogue/book/9781849054706).

Performed: seated.

Suitable for: creating an uplifting mood.

Will help with: enabling those with hearing impairments to feel included. Revisiting the signing is good for memory training. The dance helps to maintain manual dexterity, and may also be useful for reminiscence work.

Watch out for: movements above shoulders where contraindicated. Also watch out for being put off by your first glance at the movements. Take some time to practise them before you demonstrate them and teach the movements very slowly from the beginning. This dance becomes a favourite to be performed again and again. In due course you will all be rewarded by the uplifting experience of knowing the moves by heart and performing them in harmony with each other to one of the most beautiful hymns in the English language.

Music: 'Morning Has Broken' (pick a slow version).

Props: None.

Words

Morning has broken
Like the first morning,
Blackbird has spoken
Like the first bird.
Praise for the singing,
Praise for the morning,
Praise for them springing
Fresh from the Word.

Sweet the rain's new fall
Sunlit from heaven,
Like the first dew fall
On the first grass.
Praise for the sweetness
Of the wet garden,
Sprung in completeness
Where his feet pass.

Mine is the sunlight,
Mine is the morning,
Born of the one light
Eden saw play.
Praise with elation,
Praise every morning,
God's re-creation
Of the new day.

Lyrics: Eleanor Farjeon

Movements

Verse one	
Morning has broken	Start with arms bent at elbow in front of body, right forearm lies on top of left. Then with index finger of right hand pointing, open right forearm making an arc (keeping left forearm flat).
Like the	Put your two index fingers next to each other pointing away from the body, and slide them against each other, forward and back.
first	Point right index finger upwards, palm facing away from body.
morning,	Palms crossed in front, facing body, then open in an arc either side.
Blackbird has	Make a fist and pull fist down right cheek.
spoken	Fist with index finger and thumb extended, open and then close.
Like the	Put your two index fingers next to each other pointing away from the body, and slide them against each other, forward and back.
first	Point right index finger upwards, palm facing away from body.
bird.	With both fists, index finger and thumb extended, open and close, open and close finger and thumb, as you move fists away to either side of body.
Praise for the	Both fists with thumb extended upwards, slide up and down against each other.

singing,	With index finger and middle finger of each fist extended touch both sides of mouth and then extend in an arc above shoulders, including a loop in the arc if you can.
Praise for the	Both fists with thumb extended upwards, slide up and down against each other.
morning,	Palms crossed in front, facing body, then open in an arc either side.
Praise for them	Both fists with thumb extended upwards, slide up and down against each other.
springing	Arms bent at elbow across body with left forearm behind right, palms facing body. Then raise left forearm in upwards 'springing-up' gesture, and spread fingers.
Fresh from the	Right arm down, left palm, with fingers spread, moves up right arm in stroking motion.
word.	Left hand forms a fist with thumb extended and thumb draws a cross on the back of the right hand.
Verse two	
Sweet	Right fist with thumb and index finger touching make a twist at the lips.
the rain's new fall	Raise both hands in front and gently ripple downwards like rain.
Sunlit from heaven,	Raise both arms above head to the left and with palms facing down, fingers spread, make gathering motion, looking up towards hands.

Like the	Put your two index fingers next to each other pointing away from the body, and slide them against each other, forward and back.
first	Point right index finger upwards, palm facing away from body.
dew fall	Raise both hands and gently ripple downwards like rain.
On the first	Point right index finger upwards, palm facing away from body.
grass.	Ripple fingers of left hand, palm down, up and down length of right arm.
Praise for the	Both fists with thumb extended upwards, slide up and down against each other.
sweetness	Right fist with thumb and index finger touching make a twist at the right side of the mouth.
Of the wet garden,	Ripple fingers of left hand, palm down, up and down length of right arm.
Sprung in	Arms bent at elbow across body with left forearm behind right, palms facing body. Then raise left forearm in upwards 'springing-up' gesture, and spread fingers.
completeness	Palms facing inwards make 'whole', circular gesture using both arms.
Where his feet pass.	With right hand index and middle finger extended, 'walk' right hand away to the left of body.

Verse three	
Mine is the	Left palm taps chest.
sunlight,	Raise both arms above head to the left and with palms facing down, fingers spread, make gathering motion, looking up towards hands.
Mine is the	Left palm taps chest.
morning,	Palms crossed in front, facing body, then open in an arc either side.
Born of the	Palms facing each other, just less than body-width apart, move down from the waist to the knees.
one	Raise right hand in fist with index finger pointing upwards.
light	Raise right fist, above head to the right, and look up and let fist spring open, spreading fingers.
Eden saw play.	Roll an imaginary ball across your body, starting at your chest, and over your shoulder.
Praise	Both fists with thumb extended upwards, slide up and down against each other.
with elation,	Dip head, lower arms, then raise head and open arms wide, spreading fingers.
Praise	Both fists with thumb extended upwards, slide up and down against each other.
every morning,	Palms crossed in front, facing body, then open in an arc either side.

God's re-creation	Fists with knuckles facing outwards, thumbs tucked in but facing up. Holding right fist steady at waist level, left fist scoops (like scooping ice-cream) from right fist several times.
Of the new day.	Palms facing upwards, at waist-level, make wide arc with both arms in front of body in opening/ welcoming gesture.
(Repeat verse one)	

22

Can Can

Lively Dances

Choreography: Petra Hughes and Lucy Goodison

Introduction: This is a lively, light-hearted dance and familiar to most people. This version consists of simple, repetitive movements which are easy to grasp but nonetheless enlivening because of the uptempo accompaniment.

Performed: seated.

Suitable for: when energy needs raising or when spirits are already high.

Will help with: promoting a sense of fun while gently exercising legs, ankles and feet.

Watch out for: straining to match fast tempo.

Music: Any version of Offenbach's 'Can Can' will do.

Props: This can be performed with an imaginary skirt or with a specially made Can Can apron. Lace garters and finger puppets are two other possibilities.

Extra activities: You can make a simple Can Can apron that can be fixed around the waist with Velcro. Use a flowing, satin-like fabric, generously cut and hemmed with a full frill (avoid ostrich feathers). Participants rest the aprons on their laps and can swish them around to their heart's content in time with the rhythm. Likewise garters can be simply constructed from lace sewn on to strips of fabric and fixed by means of Velcro (avoid knicker elastic). Simple finger puppets (drawings of dancers with a hole at each leg for the index and middle finger to poke through) make the Can Can movement possible for those with very limited movement and help improve the mobility of the fingers.

Movements

1. Twist shoulders on the beat, for one verse.

2. Tap right toe on ground, then left toe, for one verse.

3. Hold imaginary skirt or Can Can apron in both hands and swish from side to side, for one verse.

4. Kick left leg then right leg in turn, slowly, and as high as you can for one verse (repeat as many times as you need until the music ends).

23

Charleston

Lively Dances

Choreography: Lucy Goodison and Petra Hughes

Introduction: Named after a town in South Carolina, this dance was considered provocative when it first became popular in the 1920s. It is an infectious dance, full of vitality and familiar to most people. This version consists of simple, repetitive movements which are easy to grasp but nonetheless enlivening because of the uptempo accompaniment. The basic move is a kicking movement and the types of hand and leg movements required for the Charleston make it easily adapted for seated participants.

Performed: seated.

Suitable for: when the mood needs uplifting.

Will help with: promoting a sense of fun. It also exercises hands and upper body in particular.

Watch out for: jerky movements.

Music: '(Put Another Nickel In) Music! Music! Music!' Teresa Brewer, London Records (1949).

Props: (Optional) Add headbands characteristic of the flappers, hankies and dancing sticks, and participants will have a great time. A flapper headband can be improvised simply by tying a scarf around the head to cover the forehead. Avoid using feathers. Long necklaces could be used and 'twizzled' (watch out for sharp edges).

Words

Put another nickel in
In the nickelodeon
All I want is having you
And music, music, music!

I'd do anything for you
Anything you'd want me to
All I want is kissin' you
And music, music, music!

Closer, my dear, come closer
The nicest part of any melody
Is when you're dancing so close to me!

So, put another nickel in
In the nickelodeon
All I want is lovin' you
And music, music, music!

Lyrics: Stephan Weiss and Bernie Baum

Movements

Verse one	
Put another nickel in	Elbows in, right hand up and index finger points to the right × 4.
In the nickelodeon	Elbows in, left hand up and index finger points to left × 4.
All I want is having you	Elbows in, right hand up and index finger points to the right × 4.
And music, music, music!	Elbows in, both hands up with palms facing forward and waving as body sways.
Verse two	
I'd do anything for you *Anything you'd want me to* *All I want is kissin' you*	Lift right foot up then kick, repeat with left foot, and repeat.
And music, music, music!	Elbows in, both hands up with palms facing forward and waving as body sways.
Verse three	
Closer, my dear, come closer *The nicest part of any melody*	Move bottom forward and backward, one cheek at a time, on the chair.
Is when you're dancing close *to me!*	Elbows in, both hands up with palms facing forward and waving as body sways.

Verse four	
Put another nickel in	Elbows in, right hand up and index finger points to the right × 4.
In the nickelodeon	Elbows in, left hand up and index finger points to left × 4.
All I want is lovin' you	Elbows in, right hand up and index finger points to the right × 4.
And music, music, music!	Elbows in, both hands up with palms facing forward and waving as body sways.
(Repeat verses two, three and four)	

'Pearly Shells' (Hawaiian)

Dances from Far Away

Choreography: Delia Silvester

Introduction: This is a traditional Hawaiian song translated and recorded in English in the 1960s. With simple, repetitive movements it is always popular with participants, who ask to do it again and again. This is a routine using some elements of sign language. This lovely dance is demonstrated online (http://www. jkp.com/catalogue/book/9781849054706).

Performed: seated.

Suitable for: promoting a joyful and playful mood and can help with reminiscence work. It can be the basis for a project on Hawaii.

Will help with: upper body and wrist mobility. Gentle, flowing movements may help with body awareness and re-experiencing sensuality.

Watch out for: over-stretching above the shoulders (see contraindications in Chapter 6).

Music: 'Pearly Shells', Don Ho, *Don Ho's Greatest Hits*, Reprise Records [MP3 download] 1975.

Props: (Optional) Hula/'grass' skirts, garlands and headbands of flowers made of paper or fabric.

Extra activities: Grass skirts can be made as aprons, fastening with Velcro or ties. The 'grass' can be represented by ribbons sewn to hang from the waistband. Leis or garlands of flowers to hang round the neck can consist of flowers made of soft fabrics. Sew all the flowers closely together onto a longer length of ribbon. A flower, made in the same way, can be pushed gently behind the ear too. Scrapbooks of photos of beautiful beaches, the sea and tropical island landscapes can be compiled; looking at seaside postcards can form part of reminiscence work. Handling a collection of shells (avoid using any with sharp edges) enables participants to experience texture and memory associations (shells in a bowl of lukewarm water will have a different glow or shine) and listening to recordings of the sea is great for relaxation.

Words

Pearly shells from the ocean
Shining in the sun, covering the shore
When I see them
My heart tells me that I love you
More than all the little pearly shells.

For every grain of sand upon the beach
I've got a kiss for you
And I have more left over
For the stars that twinkle in the blue.

Pearly shells from the ocean
Shining in the sun, covering the shore
When I see them
My heart tells me that I love you
More than all the little pearly shells.

Lyrics: traditional Hawaiian song with English lyrics by Webley Edwards and Leon Pober

Movements

A gentle swaying movement throughout the dance fits the Hawaiian rhythms and tradition and imitates the movement of waves. This can be maintained with a 'side, together, side, kick' step (right foot steps right, left foot joins it, right foot steps right, left foot gives a very small kick, then repeat starting with the left foot).

Verse one	
Pearly shells	Describe a big circle in front of you, as if it is the outline of a shell.
from the ocean	Gently move arms to make wave-like movements.
Shining in the sun,	Lift arms up together towards the sun and make them sway.
covering the shore	Lower arms and make pushing movements away and also drawing back in towards the body.
When I see them	Raise arms, bent at elbow to shoulder height, with hands as split fingers, pull hands away to each side from in front of the eyes.
My heart tells me that I love you	Cup hands to heart.
More than	Make a ladder movement with hands flat, held horizontal, palms down, pointing across the body, one a little above the other. Then place the lower palm above the top palm, then the new lower palm on top of that.

all the little pearly shells.	Draw semicircle with right hand to the side of the body, then add a semicircle to the left with the left hand.
Verse two	
For every grain of sand upon the beach	Lower hands in front and make the gesture of picking up handfuls of sand, feeling the grains and letting them slip through fingers as you extend your arms out to each side.
I've got a kiss for you	With left hand on hip, raise right hand and blow a kiss.
And I have more left over	Make a ladder movement with hands flat, held horizontal, palms down, pointing across the body, one a little above the other. Then place the lower palm above the top palm, then the new lower palm on top of that.
For the stars that twinkle in the blue.	Reach up first with right arm, then with left, each time making a fist, palm outwards, then letting the fist spring open, spreading fingers each time into a starburst gesture. Repeat.
(Repeat verse one)	

25

Oriental Eye Movements

Dances from Far Away

Choreography: Delia Silvester

Introduction: Many movements from the Far East have specific health-giving effects. Exercising the eyes helps to maintain good eyesight for as long as possible.

Performed: seated.

Suitable for: during the warm-up at the start of a session.

Will help with: maintaining mobility in the muscles of the face and neck and keeping eyes functioning as well as possible.

Watch out for: over-stretching the neck.

Music: anything with a Chinese or Oriental feel.

Props: (Optional) Chinese-style fans. Make sure they have no sharp points.

Extra activities: You could develop a session further from these exercises, by giving participants fans and using Chinese music as a backdrop to exploring more eye movements around the fans: everyone moving their heads the same way, fluttering the fans, peeking, making eye contact with the person in the next chair and so on. This will also exercise hands and fingers well.

Movements

1. Close and open eyes. Move eyes from side to side.

2. Without moving the head, look up, look to the sides and look down.

3. Repeat.

4. Squeeze and tighten the muscles around your eyes (by screwing up your face).

5. Then let go.

6. Breathe in slowly. Breathe out slowly.

7. Turn your head gently, look to your right and then look as far back as you can. (Don't overstretch or go beyond what is comfortable.)

8. Repeat the movement to your left.

9. Tilt your neck/head towards your right shoulder.

10. Tilt your neck/head towards your left shoulder.

11. Neck towards your right, oblique position.

12. Neck towards your left, oblique position.

26

'Haul Away Joe'

Sea shanties and songs about the sea

Choreography: Petra Hughes and Lucy Goodison

Introduction: This is a sea shanty that many participants may remember.

Performed: standing or seated.

Suitable for: reminiscence work and for work around a project about the sea.

Will help with: maintaining mobility in the upper body.

Watch out for: raising the hands too high, over-stretching or aching arms.

Music: 'Haul Away Joe', Clancy Brothers and Tommy Makem, *In Person At Carnegie Hall*, Sony Music Entertainment (2009).

Props: (Optional) A short length of soft rope for each participant; scarves tied around heads in pirate fashion.

Words

When I was a little boy so my mother told me,
Way haul away, we'll haul away Joe.

That if I did not kiss the girls, my lips would all grow mouldy,
Way haul away, we'll haul away Joe.

Way haul away, the good ship now is rolling,
Way haul away, we'll haul away Joe.

King Louis was the king of France before the revolution,
Way haul away, we'll haul away Joe.

And then he got his head cut off, it spoiled his constitution,
Way haul away, we'll haul away Joe.

First I met a Yankee girl and she was fat and lazy,
Way haul away, we'll haul away Joe.

Then I met an Irish girl, she damn near drove me crazy,
Way haul away, we'll haul away Joe.

Way haul away, we're bound for better weather,
Way haul away, we'll haul away Joe.

Lyrics: traditional

Movements

For this dance participants need to imagine pulling on an imaginary rope as if hauling in sails.

When I was a little boy so my mother told me,	Hands on thighs or hips and sway from side to side.
Way haul away, we'll haul away Joe.	Right foot outstretched and pull as if on a rope from the right, repeat to the left.
That if I did not kiss the girls, my lips would all grow mouldy,	Throw a kiss then cover lips with hands, open hands and pull a face.
Way haul away, we'll haul away Joe.	Right foot outstretched and pull as if on a rope from the right, repeat to the left.
Way haul away, the good ship now is rolling,	Pull the rope and then roll the arms around each other.
Way haul away, we'll haul away Joe.	Right foot outstretched and pull as if on a rope from the right, repeat to the left.
King Louis was the king of France before the revolution,	Put on an imaginary crown and fold arms smugly.
Way haul away, we'll haul away Joe.	Right foot outstretched and pull as if on a rope from the right, repeat to the left.
And then he got his head cut off, it spoiled his constitution,	Cup the chin with both hands and pull a face, then hands on tummy as if it's aching.

Way haul away, we'll haul away Joe.	Right foot outstretched and pull as if on a rope from the right, repeat to the left.
First I met a Yankee girl	Rock alternate shoulders back and forth and with right hand make a cute wave.
and she was fat and lazy,	Make fat, heavy, wide stamps.
Way haul away, we'll haul away Joe.	Right foot outstretched and pull as if on a rope from the right, repeat to the left.
Then I met an Irish girl,	Rock alternate shoulders back and forth and with right hand make a cute wave.
she damn near drove me crazy,	Arms and hands straight down the sides to make a thin body then tap with toes in Irish dancing style.
Way haul away, we'll haul away Joe.	Right foot outstretched and pull as if on a rope from the right, repeat to the left.
Way haul away, we're bound for better weather,	Pull as if on a rope, then lift rope to shoulder height stretched between hands and sway.
Way haul away, we'll haul away Joe.	Right foot outstretched and pull as if on a rope from the right, repeat to the left.

27

'Shenandoah'

Sea Shanties and Songs About the Sea

Choreography: Lucy Goodison and Petra Hughes

Introduction: This is an American folk song that many participants may remember singing in childhood. Its provenance is unknown: some say it tells the story of a roving trader in love with the daughter of a Native American chief telling of his intention to take the girl west with him across the Missouri river; others say the song tells of a pioneer's nostalgia for the Shenandoah River Valley in Virginia, or of a Confederate soldier in the American Civil War dreaming of his home in Virginia. The song is also associated with escaped slaves who were said to sing the song in gratitude because the river allowed their scent to be lost.

Performed: seated.

Suitable for: quiet groups of individuals with limited movement, quiet times.

Will help with: soothing and calming and promoting a mood of nostalgia.

Watch out for: participants choosing suitable scarves; very short, light scarves are best for those with very limited strength in their arms. Within that limitation, it is a good idea to let participants choose a scarf that appeals to them.

Music: 'Shenandoah', Paul Robeson, *The Best of Paul Robeson*, [CD] Music Digital (2003).

Props: Chiffon or light satin scarves in blue and sea-green of ideally one metre in length. Larger lengths of fabric in the same colours could be used by activities coordinators to create a river down the centre of the room or, with each participant holding on, enable participants to dance together.

Words

O Shenandoah, I long to hear you,
Away, you rollin' river,
O Shenandoah, I long to hear you,
Away I'm bound to go 'cross the wide Missouri.

O Shenandoah, I took a notion,
Away, you rollin' river,
To sail across the stormy ocean.
Away I'm bound to go 'cross the wide Missouri.

'Tis seven long years since last I see thee,
Away, you rollin' river,
'Tis seven long years since last I see thee,
Away I'm bound to go 'cross the wide Missouri.

O Shenandoah, I long to hear you,
Away, you rollin' river,
O Shenandoah, I long to hear you,
Away I'm bound to go 'cross the wide Missouri.

Lyrics: traditional

Movements

Verse one	
O Shenandoah, I long to hear you,	Bundle up scarf, tilt head and rest cheek on scarf like a pillow. Draw knees together, raise feet to tiptoe and rock gently; the body closes up in an expression of yearning.
Away, you rollin' river,	Shake out scarf to full length in front; the feeling is one of letting go.
O Shenandoah, I long to hear you,	As before, rest cheek on scarf like a pillow.
Away I'm bound to go	Hold each end of scarf and make forward circles as if rowing – one or two circles.
'cross the wide Missouri.	Pull scarf taut between hands, arms out straight in front of body.
Verse two	
O Shenandoah, I took a notion,	Hold scarf out then bring it in to the heart.
Away, you rollin' river,	Shake out scarf to full length in front; the feeling is one of letting go.
To sail across the stormy ocean,	Hold one end of scarf and spin it energetically from the wrist in windmill-like circles in front of the body, extending each foot forward alternately; the feeling is one of energy and expansion.

Away I'm bound to go	Hold each end of scarf and make forward circles as if rowing – one or two circles.
'cross the wide Missouri.	Pull scarf taut between hands, arms out straight in front of body, or held low resting on the knees.
Verse three	
'Tis seven long years since last I see thee,	Hold one end of scarf in right hand and pull the length of it slowly through the loose fist of the left hand. If that is not possible, pull scarf slowly over the back of the wrist; feeling of extent/length of time.
Away, you rollin' river,	Shake out scarf to full length in front; the feeling is one of letting go.
'Tis seven long years since last I see thee,	As before, hold one end of scarf in right hand and pull the length of it slowly through the loose fist of the left hand.
Away I'm bound to go	Hold each end of scarf and make forward circles as if rowing – one or two circles.
'cross the wide Missouri.	Pull scarf taut between hands, arms out straight in front of body, or held low resting on the knees.
(Repeat first verse)	

28

'What Shall We Do with the Drunken Sailor?'(Create a Dance)

Sea Shanties and Songs about the Sea

Choreography: Lucy Goodison and Petra Hughes

Introduction: This sea shanty is very repetitive and so well known that it presents an ideal opportunity for the activity coordinator and participants to work together to create a dance.

Performed: standing or seated.

Suitable for: a group active enough to pick up movement ideas and respond to others in the group.

Will help with: reminiscence work as many people learn this song in childhood. Participants will experience it as empowering to lead a movement that everyone else follows. They will connect with each other through following each other's movements and this encourages empathetic communication.

Watch out for: movements that are too ambitious for some in the group.

Music: Any version of the song will do, it doesn't matter if the words or verses are a bit different.

Props: Scarves could be tied pirate-fashion around heads.

Words

VERSE ONE
What shall we do with the drunken sailor?
What shall we do with the drunken sailor?
What shall we do with the drunken sailor?
Early in the morning.

[Chorus]

Way, hey and up she rises,
Way, hey and up she rises,
Way, hey and up she rises
Early in the morning.

VERSE TWO
Shave his belly with a rusty razor,
Shave his belly with a rusty razor,
Shave his belly with a rusty razor
Early in the morning.

[Chorus]

VERSE THREE
Put him in the hold with the Captain's daughter,
Put him in the hold with the Captain's daughter,
Put him in the hold with the Captain's daughter
Early in the morning.

[Chorus]

VERSE FOUR
Put him in the scupper with the hosepipe on him,
Put him in the scupper with the hosepipe on him,
Put him in the scupper with the hosepipe on him
Early in the morning.

[Chorus]

VERSE FIVE
Put him in the longboat till he's sober,
Put him in the longboat till he's sober,
Put him in the longboat till he's sober
Early in the morning.

[Chorus]

VERSE SIX
That's what we do with the drunken sailor,
That's what we do with the drunken sailor,
That's what we do with the drunken sailor
Early in the morning.

Lyrics: traditional

Movements
Step one (preparation)

You could start by asking, 'What sailor movements can you think of? Hornpipe movements?' Pick up movements suggested by participants and repeat them for the rest to join in. When participants run out of ideas, or if none are forthcoming, run through the following movements, talking about what they are each time:

- pulling the rope from one side to the other

- arms folded, tilting from side to side (hornpipe movement)

- feet tapping in 1-2-3 rhythm (hornpipe movement)

- arm movements as if climbing up netting

- shading eyes as if scanning a distant horizon at sea, first left side, then right

- pulling up flag

- hosing down the deck

- one arm out to side, the other hand touches inner elbow of that arm; swap arms

- elbows out to side, fingertips touching in the middle, swing hands up until they are above elbows (this is close to sign language for morning, suggesting sunrise)

- moving fists back and forth as if scrubbing the deck.

Step two

Ask the participants if they can remember any of the movements; see if they can show any of them. When someone performs a movement, encourage the rest of the group to join in and follow suit. Then ask someone else for a movement and all join in again. You could work around the circle asking people in turn.

Step three

Put the music on and choose one of the movements for the first verse and demonstrate it. Encourage them all to join in.

Step four

For the chorus, choose one of the movements that feels appropriate and do it throughout the chorus, for example, pulling up the flag, and encourage everyone to join in.

Step five

Say, 'OK, now it's your turn to choose the movements. You remember the movements? You can always make one up if you want to.' Choose someone to start who will lead during the next verse, and encourage everyone to join in with them. After a few repetitions of the movement, encourage that person to point to another person to lead during the next bit, and everyone follows the second person, who then points to the next person, and so on. If one of the participants can't think of a movement, prompt them.

Step six

If the group is really interested and involved you can facilitate them to work together and agree a finished version of the dance, selecting specific moves they prefer for each verse, moves that fit the words. Then the group can perform the whole song through together with this, their own choreography, and can return to it on future occasions.

29

Hand Jive

Dances Popular in the Twentieth Century

Choreography: Lucy Goodison and Petra Hughes

Introduction: This is a popular novelty dance that started in the UK in the 1950s. Since all the movements are with the arms, it is ideal for seated participants.

Performed: seated.

Suitable for: having fun and creating a lively, participatory mood.

Will help with: maintaining arm and finger mobility. It also gives memory training as people remember the sequence. Encouraging participants to create their own movements fosters confidence and involvement.

Watch out for: participants creating arm movements that may be contraindicated for others to follow.

Music: Johnny Otis's 'Willie and the Hand Jive' (1958) is the song that popularised the dance in the USA, and Eric Clapton does a version of it on his album *461 Ocean Boulevard* (1974) which is ideal. But any rock number with a slow beat will work; for example, 'Rock Around the Clock' is fine if you use alternate beats so that the movements don't have to be done too fast.

Props: None.

Movements

You can do the four best-known basic movements one after the other:

1. Put left fingers on bottom of right elbow. Hold lower right arm vertical and make a circle with the index finger. Continue with this movement in time with the music until everyone has 'got' it. Then reverse the arms and repeat.

2. Hold your hands out horizontally in front of you, one a few inches above the other, with the palms facing down, and cross them and uncross them with a horizontal slicing movement. Put the lower one above the higher one and repeat. Again, continue with the movement until everyone can do it before moving on.

3. Hold your hands in front of you with the thumb uppermost and the palms facing you, one hand in front of the other. Circle them round each other, making the shape of a wheel going forward in front of you.

4. Make your hands into fists with the thumb uppermost. Bounce your right fist lightly on top of your left fist several times, then reverse.

Allow plenty of time for each movement and carry on doing it, in time to the music, until everyone has grasped it before you move on to the next movement. When you have done all four movements, run the sequence through again.

Creating additional movements

When participants have mastered all four movements, ask if anyone can remember any more. For example, quite a few people remember the 'hitch hiking' gesture, or slapping the thighs with both hands. Then ask if anyone can invent their own. It could be something simple like a clap. Whatever movements participants come up with, pick out one of them, copy it and get all the others to join in. Then you can ask, 'Has anyone else got another one?' and do the same with another participant's movement.

It is empowering for a group member to see others following a move that they have initiated, so the more people contribute moves, the better it is for the group.

Sometimes you can go round the circle, asking each person in turn for a movement. If someone feels shy or gestures to the effect that they can't think of one, take that gesture (maybe a shrug, or a wave away, or clasping their hands together) and repeat it as a move for everyone to follow in time to the music.

You may want to put the track on again, start with the well-known movements, then carry on through the track using in turn all the moves that group members have contributed, encouraging them to jog your memory if necessary.

30

Line Dancing

Dances Popular in the Twentieth Century

Choreography: Lucy Goodison

Introduction: Line dancing has links to folk dancing but nowadays is usually performed to country and western music. Usually, participants all face the same direction in rows, although performing it in a circle is fine. Dancers don't touch each other and everyone performs in unison the same sequence of steps, with turns and claps included.

Performed: seated or standing with a walking frame.

Suitable for: raising spirits and energy in the group.

Will help with: maintaining mobility in feet and ankles. Using cowboy hats ensures movement of the upper body too.

Watch out for: the usual contraindications, especially twisting any part of the body too much to the side.

Music: Any cheerful country and western track with a slow, strong beat.

Props: (Optional) Cowboy hats.

Extra activities: Group singing of well-known cowboy songs like 'Home on the Range', 'Yellow Rose of Texas', 'O Susanna', 'The Ballad of Davy Crockett'.

Movements

Choose a few of these moves that your participants can enjoy doing, and arrange them in a set order to form a short sequence that can be repeated in unison. The easier ones are listed first.

1. Step on right foot, then on left foot, then on right foot, then clap once (four counts).

2. Step on left foot, then on right foot, then on left foot, then clap once (four counts).

3. With hands on hips sway upper torso, leaning to right then to left in turn (eight counts).

4. Right foot on ground with toe forward. Lift toe and turn it out at an angle to the side and back. Repeat four times. Do the same with the left foot and repeat four times.

5. Clap hands on the right side of the body four times. Clap hands on the left side of the body four times.

6. Move right foot forward diagonally and put it down. Left foot joins it. Move right foot forward diagonally and put it down. Left foot points toe on ground beside right foot.

    Move left foot backwards again diagonally and put it down. Right foot joins it. Move left foot backwards again diagonally and put it down. Right foot points toe on ground beside left foot.

    Repeat this whole step with both the forwards and backwards movement four times.

    You can repeat the sequence on the other side, starting with the left foot moving forward diagonally.

7. If you have hats, looking straight ahead, take cowboy hat from head with both hands and hold it in front of your body with the top away from your body. Slide it to the right and lean to the right, slide it to the left and lean to the left, bring it back to the centre and put it back on head.

8. Clap in front of your body four times, then wiggle your torso for four counts. (You can have a bit of fun with this one!)

9. Move right foot to right side to tap the right heel on the ground then replace foot. Repeat to the left.

    Move right foot to right side to tap right heel twice on the ground then replace foot. Repeat to left.

Move right foot to right side to tap right heel three times on the ground then replace foot. Repeat to left. Move right foot to right side to tap right heel four times on the ground then replace foot. Repeat to left. Clap four times – if you managed to keep the count you deserve it!

31

The Waltz

Dances Popular in the Twentieth Century

Choreography: Lucy Goodison and Petra Hughes

Introduction: The waltz, a dance with a 1-2-3 rhythm where couples hold each other close, has a long history and was considered shocking in Germany and Austria in the eighteenth century. Many older people will remember dancing it in their youth.

Performed: seated.

Suitable for: creating a gentle, nostalgic, even romantic mood.

Will help with: giving the whole body gentle exercise, especially helping flexibility of the torso, as well as inspiring reminiscence work.

Watch out for: holding arms too high, or holding them out in front too long, causing pressure.

Music: Any slow waltz with a clear 1-2-3 rhythm. A well-known tune like 'The Blue Danube' will help to engage participants.

Props: (Optional) Fabric roses to hold in hand or put in hair. Feather boas (not real feathers, but lengths of feather fabric, which is not too expensive).

Extra activities: Making roses to serve as props. Reminiscence about occasions when participants danced the waltz earlier in life.

Movements

The waltz is very much a dance for two, but this version is for one. You could introduce it by saying, 'We don't need partners. We can waltz all by ourselves. We can imagine a ballroom setting.'

It is best to teach the movements for the top and bottom halves of the body separately, then put them together and add the arm movements.

Upper body movements: sway the upper body from the waist, first to the right, then to the left. Do this to the count of 1-2-3, always moving to the side on the count of '1'. Put feeling into it, imagining you are swaying to and fro with a partner.

Lower body movements: these involve marking out the 1-2-3 tempo with your feet, starting with the right foot and slowly at first.

(1) Move your right foot to the right, (2) bring left foot to join it, then (3) raise right foot and put it down again.

Repeat on the other side, that is, (1) move left foot to left, (2) bring right foot to join it, then (3) raise left foot and put it down again.

The emphasis is always on the '1', and the other two counts follow more swiftly. Practise these foot movements in time with the music, then combine them with the torso movement so that the upper body sways to the right as the right foot steps to the right, and the same to the left.

Now add in the arms: make a circle in front of you with your arms and clasp your hands together in front of you with the palms facing towards you. Raise your arms as high as is comfortable up to shoulder height to represent your dance partner facing you as you sway and move your feet. Practise doing the swaying, feet, and arms all together.

When participants have mastered these basic movements, you can encourage them to maintain the swaying and the foot movements but vary their arm position and make any nostalgic, lavish, romantic or expressive gestures that they feel like making in time to the music. Any Fred and Ginger film will suggest reaching, wave-like, wafting or stroking movements that you could model for the group members to get them started. (Remind them to lower their arms and/or rest them on their legs as and when they get tired.)

32

Free/Creative Dance

Dances Popular in the Twentieth Century

Choreography: Lucy Goodison

Introduction: It is very good for people whose lives are mostly organised by others, as the lives of the fragile elderly often are, to create something for themselves. Creative dance gives an opportunity for inventiveness and self-expression. A number of different frameworks can be used, but here the themes of the four elements – earth, air, fire and water – are suggested to encourage people to explore different qualities of movement.

Performed: seated or standing, with or without a walking frame for support, as appropriate.

Suitable for: when people are already well warmed-up and feeling responsive, to give them an opportunity to be creative on their own initiative.

Will help with: gaining feelings of confidence, autonomy and satisfaction. Also, sometimes participants communicate with one another more through the dance than they do in day-to-day life.

Watch out for: group members being too shy to get started moving on their own initiative. It usually helps if you join in yourself, and interact with others to help them get involved. At the start, remind participants not to go beyond the limits of comfortable movements.

Music: For the four themes of earth, air, fire and water, here are some suggestions:

- Earth: 'Diamonds on the Soles of Her Shoes' from Paul Simon's album *Graceland*.

- Air: Something light from the Modern Jazz Quartet.

- Fire: Stravinsky's 'The Firebird'.

- Water: Handel's 'Water Music'.

You may prefer to choose something yourself that creates the right mood for you.

Props: Filmy red scarves to be flames; soft blue scarves to be water. Scarves should always be light and not too long, ideally in jewel-like colours and fabrics pleasing to the touch.

Extra activities: During arts and crafts activities, group members could be given colours and paper to do a picture, or pictures, expressing how they felt while they were listening to the music and moving to the mood of the different elements.

Movements

You can just put the music on, suggest the theme and leave people to move however they want. Or you could make it easier for them to get started by demonstrating some movements on the theme yourself. Or you could help people get into the mood and lead them into it by speaking words to create a picture, atmosphere and ideas for them at the start. Below are some suggestions along these lines on the theme of the four elements (remember to leave plenty of space between the phrases where there are dots (…) so that participants have time to absorb the words and move on their own).

Earth: Imagine you are walking into a garden. With bare feet on soft grass. You can feel it under your feet. Let your feet wriggle and stretch gently… Explore what other movements your feet can make… And your legs… You can shift your weight in your chair… Feel your body's connection with the earth, and the power that is in the earth… Imagine the earth is sending up strength into your body… Now I'm going to leave the music on and you can let your whole body move with those earthy qualities of solidity and strength… Move any way that feels comfortable for you…

Air: In that same garden, see if you can picture a tall tree, gently swaying in the wind. Imagine the top of that tree, way up in the air. You could rock your torso gently like that tree… Let your arms move a little too… And your fingers, move them as if they were leaves and a little breeze was passing through them… So light, like the air… Imagine your whole body light and floating, moving in the air… Your arms and legs too… Moving in the breeze… Now, with the music, carry on exploring how many ways your body can move as light as the air…

Fire: Now you've come down to earth again in the garden, and beside the tree there's a bonfire. Imagine you're looking at it, it's burning brightly and the flames are dancing… Now put your hand on your stomach and imagine there's a fire burning inside you, giving you lots of energy… Slide your hand up to your midriff, imagine the fire spreading up through your body… It's filling you with warmth. Let your body move a little with that warmth… Then a little bit more… Imagine you're moving like the spirit of the fire… (*Give out red scarves.*) Now explore ways of moving with the scarves like the fire… It might be glowing, it might be flickering, it might be flaring up… Carry on with the music and the scarves… Let the fire give you ideas, let your body play like the fire…

Water: Now, imagine rain starting. It puts out the fire. Lovely warm summer rain. You are going to let yourself get into a lovely pool of warm water… Let your whole body relax and stretch in the water… Washing away all your tensions… Let your whole body relax and stretch in the water… Flowing this way and that… (*Give out blue scarves.*) Imagine the scarf is like the water, moving gently…

Stroking your body... You can let yourself sway in the current... Now carry on with the music and let your body do what it wants to do in the lovely water... gently stretching, bending, so smooth and relaxing, however it wants to move...

Afterwards, you could invite people to talk about how they felt in the different elements, and whether any memories or thoughts arose for them during the dancing.

About the Author

Delia Silvester was born in 1940 in Davao City in the Philippines, where she became first a ballet dancer and then later a fully trained PE instructor. She continued her training in the UK after meeting and marrying her husband Nigel and returning to England with him. Wanting to contribute to the new culture she found herself in, Delia worked for the Royal National Institute for Deaf People (RNID) and the British Nursing Association, among others, and through outreach work in care homes, developed a series of movements-to-music and dances specifically designed to address the mobility and memory limitations of the frail elderly. Over a period of 11 years she refined her teaching and ran workshops training activities coordinators on behalf of NAPA in south-west England. In 2004, Delia created and led Dance Doctors, a small dance company that performed in care settings, teaching both residents and activities coordinators. This book, which Delia was determined to complete before she died on the last day of 2011, shares a lifetime's knowledge, dedication and experience of the benefits of dance, all underwritten by her conviction: 'if it aches, move it!'

About the editor

Susan Frampton has worked in the magazine and book publishing industries for over 30 years as a publisher and editor.

About Dance Doctors

Lucy Goodison PhD, MFPhys (Massage and Physiology), Registered Dance Movement Therapist, has worked professionally with massage and creative movement for over 30 years. She has also taught in the adult education service and is the author of books and articles on history, psychotherapy, mental health and disability. She joined Dance Doctors in 2004.

Petra Hughes BA (Creative Arts), QTLS (PGCE in Art, Dance and Forest School) first learnt leading of movement to music for elderly and disabled people with Seona Ross in 1988. She has performed creative and ethnic movement with The World Tree, Theme Traders, Magical Experiences and Romanska. She has led dance sessions part-time in care settings in Dorset since 2002, helped to form Dance Doctors and currently leads in movement and singing at Tree Tops Care Home and for the Knees Up structured programme for mature people.

Dance Doctors was Delia's brainchild. She started the group in 2004 to work with other dancers in combining performance with participatory movement during sessions at residential and nursing homes in Dorset. Typically, a session would include a warm-up, a costumed performance (e.g. Charleston, tap or Hawaiian dance) and then a focus on teaching aspects of the dance to residents, tailored to their level of mobility. The dance would then be performed again with the participation of the audience. If time permitted, other dances would follow. Most of the dances in Part 3 have been tried and tested in this way.

Calendar for Themed Sessions

A calendar of events, festivals and special days (dates may vary from year to year).

January

1	New Year's Day
6	Epiphany (Christian, commemorating the arrival of the Three Wise Men)
25	Burn's Night
26	Australia Day
27	Holocaust Memorial Day
28	Royal National Lifeboat Institution (RNLI) SOS (fundraising) Day
29	National Storytelling Week
29	Royal Society for the Protection of Birds (RSPB) Big Garden Birdwatch
	World Religion Day (third Sunday)

February

2	Chinese New Year
	Candlemas (Christian)
	Shrove Tuesday / Pancake Day / Mardi Gras
	Ash Wednesday (day after Shrove Tuesday)
14	Valentine's Day

17   World Community Arts Day
     National Pub Week

March

1   St David's Day (patron saint of Wales)
5   St Piran's Day (Cornwall)
     World Book Day (first Thursday)
8   International Women's Day
     Commonwealth Day (second Monday)
17   St Patrick's Day (patron saint of Ireland)
18   Wildlife Week
21   World Poetry Day
21   World Forestry Day
     Mother's Day
22   World Day for Water
25   Greek Independence Day
27   World Theatre Day
     Red Nose Day

April

1   April Fool's Day
     Maundy Thursday
     Good Friday
     Easter Sunday
7   World Health Day
21   Queen's birthday
22   Earth Day
23   St George's Day (patron saint of England)
29   International Dance Day

May

1   May Day

2   Deaf Awareness Week

3   World Press Freedom Day

8   World Red Cross/Red Crescent Day

9   Europe Day

15 National Smile Month (oral health awareness)

20 Cultural Diversity Day

22 Buddha's birthday

23 National Vegetarian Week

    Share a Story Month

June

2   Anniversary of the Coronation of Queen Elizabeth II

4   Heart Week

5   World Environment Day

8   World Oceans Day

21 Summer Solstice

24 Midsummer's Day (Druids)

29 Armed Forces Day

    Father's Day

30 International Festival of the Seas

July

1   Canada Day

4   American Independence Day

14 Festival of British Archaeology

28 National Marine Week

August

1   Great British Beer Festival

4   Edinburgh Tattoo

12   International Youth Day

15   Independence Day India

       Notting Hill Carnival (August Bank Holiday)

September

8   Heritage Open Days

13   Yom Kippur (Jewish)

21   International Day of Peace

29   World Heart Day

26   European Day of Languages

       Chinese Moon/Lantern Festival

       Harvest Festival (Christian)

October

1   International Day for Older People

1   China National Day

4   Ramadan (Muslim) begins

       Pearly Kings and Queens (first Sunday)

5   World Teachers' Day

6   Mad Hatter's Day

4   National Poetry Day

8   British Food Fortnight

       World Sight Day (second Thursday)

       Grandparents' Day (first Sunday)

16   World Food Day

21   Apple Day

21   Trafalgar Day

24   United Nations Day

31   Halloween

Breast Awareness Month

November

1   Diwali (Hindu, festival with lights)

1   All Saints' Day (Christian)

2   All Souls' Day (Christian)

4   Mischief Night

5   Bonfire Night

11   Armistice Day

Remembrance Sunday

13   National Kindness Day

23   National Tree Week

Thanksgiving Day (fourth Sunday)

30   St Andrew's Day (patron saint of Scotland)

December

6   St Nicholas's Day (Christian)

21   Winter Solstice

24   Christmas Eve

25   Christmas Day

26   Boxing Day

31   New Year's Eve

Organisations

Age UK: www.ageuk.org.uk

Aged Care Australia: www.agedcareaustralia.gov.au

Alzheimer Society Canada: www.alzheimer.ca

Alzheimer's Association (USA): www.alz.org

Alzheimer's Australia: www.fightdementia.org.au

Alzheimer's Society (UK): www.alzheimers.org.uk

Arthritis Care: www.arthritiscare.org.uk

Arts Council England: www.artscouncil.org.uk

Association for Dance Movement Psychotherapy UK (ADMP): www.admt.org.uk

Australia Council for the Arts: www.australiacouncil.gov.au/artforms/dance

Canada Council for the Arts: www.canadacouncil.ca/dance/

CARP (Canada): www.carp.ca

Dementia Services Development Centre, University of Stirling: www.dementia.stir.ac.uk (accessed February 2012)

Elder Care (USA): www.eldercare.gov

EXTEND: www.extend.org.uk

Foundation for Community Dance: www.communitydance.org.uk

National Association for Providers of Activities for Older People (NAPA): www.napa-activities.co.uk

National Endowment for the Arts (USA): www.arts.gov

Nutrition Australia: www.nutritionaustralia.org

Performing Rights Society for Music (PRS): www.prsformusic.com (accessed March 2012)

Public Performance Licence (PPL): www.ppluk.com (accessed March 2012)

Stroke Association: www.stroke.org.uk

Bibliography

Best, C., van Wijck, F., Dinan-Young, S. *et al.* (2010). *Best Practice Guidance for the Development of Exercise after Stroke Services in Community Settings.* Edinburgh: University of Edinburgh. Available: http://www.exerciseafterstroke.org.uk/resources/Exercise_After_Stroke_Guidelines.pdf (accessed 19 July 2013).

British Heart Foundation (2008). *Active for Later Life: Promoting Physical Activity with Older People.* London: British Heart Foundation.

Coaten, R. (2001). 'Exploring Reminiscence through Dance and Movement', *Journal of Dementia Care*, 9, 5: 19–22.

Cotterell, L. ed. (1989). *100 Favourite Poems.* London: Piatkus.

Crichton, S. (1997). 'Moving Is the Language I Use—Communication Is My Goal', *Journal of Dementia Care*, 5, 6: 16–17.

Donald, J. and Hall, S. (1999). 'Dance: the Getting There Group', *Journal of Dementia Care*, 7, 3: 24–27.

Duncan, I. (1988). *My Life.* London: Cardinal/Sphere. (First published 1928.)

Fonteyn, M. (1979). *The Magic of Dance.* New York: Alfred A. Knopf.

Gillies, B. (1997). 'The Experience of Dementia', *Journal of Dementia Care*, 5, 6: 26.

Goodill, S. W. (2005). *An Introduction to Medical Dance/Movement Therapy: Health Care in Motion.* London: Jessica Kingsley Publishers.

Harrison, C. (1985). *Dancing Circles.* With dance notes and illustrations by Janet McCrickard. Available: https://sites.google.com/site/circledancedcmetroarea/new-introductory-class/session-1 (accessed 16 August 2013).

Hayes, J. with Povey, S. (2011). *The Creative Arts in Dementia Care.* London: Jessica Kingsley Publishers.

Heymanson, C. (2009). 'Linking Hands in Circle Dance', *Journal of Dementia Care*, 17, 1: 13–14.

Hill, H. (2001). *Invitation to the Dance: Dance for People with Dementia and Their Carers*, 2nd edn. Stirling: University of Stirling.

Hughill, S. (ed.) (1961). *Shanties from the Seven Seas: Shipboard Work-Songs and Songs Used as Work-Songs from the Great Days of Sail.* London: Routledge & Kegan Paul.

Hulme, C., Wright, J., Crocker, T. *et al.* (2010). 'Non-pharmacological Approaches for Dementia that Informal Carers Might Try or Access: A Systematic Review', *International Journal of Geriatric Psychiatry*, 25, 7: 756–63.

Hunter, J. (2002). *Sacred Festivals.* London: MQ Publications.

Jaaniste, J. (2011). 'Dramatherapy and Spirituality in Dementia Care', *Dramatherapy*, 33, 1: 16–27.

Jerome, D. (1999). 'Circles of the Mind', *Journal of Dementia Care*, 7, 3: 20–24.

Jonas, G. (1992). *Dancing: The Pleasure, Power, and Art of Movement*. New York: Harry N. Abrams.

Kindell, J. and Amans, D. (2003). 'Doing Things Differently: Dance in Dementia Care', *Journal of Dementia Care*, 11, 2: 18–20.

Lamont, J. (2008). 'Remembering the Dance', *Journal of Dementia Care*, 16, 2: 11.

Lantin, B. (2010) 'Dance and Drama Workshops Helping Dementia Sufferers', *The Times*, 16 March 2010.

Lievesley, N. (2010). 'The Future Ageing of the Ethnic Minority Population of England & Wales'. London: Centre for Policy on Ageing and Runnymede Trust.

Masefield, J. (1912). *Salt-Water Poems and Ballads*. London: Macmillan.

Palgrave, F. T. (ed.) (1950). *The Golden Treasury of the Best Songs and Lyrical Poems in the English Language*. London: Macmillan.

Perrin, T. (1998). 'Lifted into a World of Rhythm and Melody', *Journal of Dementia Care*, 6, 1: 22–24.

Pruszynski, J. A., King, G. L., Boisse, L., *et al.* (2010). 'Stimulus-Locked Responses on Human Arm Muscles Reveal a Rapid Neural Pathway Linking Visual Input to Motor Arm Output', *European Journal of Neuroscience*, 32, 6: 1049–57.

Rippon, H. (1975). *Discovering English Folk Dance*. Oxford: Shire Publications.

Schneider, J. and Mann, A. (1997). 'Depression and Dementia in Care Homes', *Journal of Dementia Care*, 5, 6: 27.

Sorell, W. (1967) *The Dance. Through the Ages*. London: Thames and Hudson.

Steinman, L. (1986). *The Knowing Body: Elements of Contemporary Performance and Dance*. Boston and London: Shambhala.

Stolenzenburg, M. (c.1979). *Exploring Mime*. New York: Sterling Publishing.

Violets, M. (2000). 'An Experiential View of Dance Movement Therapy'. In: D. Aldridge (ed.) *Music Therapy in Dementia Care*, 212–28. London: Jessica Kingsley Publishers.

Wosien, M.-G. (1974). *Sacred Dance: Encounter with the Gods*. New York: Avon Books.

Index